RESULTS BY DESIGN

SURVIVAL SKILLS FOR PROJECT MANAGERS

MARY DOSSETT   JULIA MALLORY

Telos
PUBLICATIONS
Huntington Beach, California

Published By:
Telos Publications
P.O. Box 4457, Huntington Beach, California 92605-4457
Toll Free 1-866-416-8973 / Phone 1-714-668-1818 / Fax 1-714-668-1100
http://www.telospublications.com

Understanding Yourself and Others is a registered trademark of Telos Publications, Fountain Valley, California.

MBTI and *Myers-Briggs Type Indicator* are trademarks or registered trademarks of the Myers-Briggs Type Indicator Trust in the United States and other countries.

PRINTED IN THE UNITED STATES OF AMERICA

International Standard Book Number: 0-9743751-0-1

Cover/Layout Design/Illustrations: Visibility Designs

Library of Congress Cataloging-in-Publication Data

Dossett, Mary.
  Results by design : survival skills for project managers / Mary Dossett, Julia Mallory.
    p. cm.
  Includes bibliographical references.
  ISBN 0-9743751-0-1 (hardcover)
  1. Project management. I. Mallory, Julia. II. Title.
  HD69.P75.D67 2004
  658.4'04--dc22
                                2004021026

From Mary

To Diane, the first project manager I ever worked with, and simply the best. Mentor and coach, at work and in life – my dear friend, you continue to be an inspiration.

From Julia

To my lovely daughters, Courtney, Christine, and Casey: thank you for choosing me as your mom. And to Dr. Linda V. Berens, who changed my life and the lives of so many others. You make a difference.

Contents

Welcome

Why write a book on project management and temperament?

During the span of two separate careers, two women of very different backgrounds made some fundamental observations:

- Project teams rarely lack the subject matter expertise they need to succeed.
- Although projects may be challenged with less than desired levels of time, resources, and money, some teams succeed while others fail miserably.
- Companies want and need their projects to succeed—they don't intentionally set them up to fail.

When Julia Mallory and Mary Dossett had the opportunity to meet and compare notes, they quickly came to the same conclusion: Project management skills combined with subject matter skills are only two-thirds of the equation. Strong "people skills," applied directly to the discipline of project management, are what distinguish the highest performing teams from their contemporaries.

These high-impact teams are typically well trained both in their subject matter areas and in project management. They most often come by the people skills intuitively, much like some people intuitively understand computers better than others. They deliver the highest levels of performance when both the project manager and the project team share the same set of values. These teams are unconsciously competent in human interactions.

Julia, a recognized authority in temperament theory, and Mary, a well known expert in project management methodology, believed that it was both necessary and possible to identify and teach the skill set necessary to master human interactions in the context of a project. They wished to turn what are typically considered "soft skills" into hard skills by presenting them side by side with a project management methodology—showing individuals and teams how to act and, more importantly, interact with each other as predictable project pressure points surface. Their goal was to integrate temperament theory into the structure and discipline of project management methodology.

This book is the result of their subsequent collaboration—a unique blend of project management and temperament. It is an attempt to integrate theory and practice from two very different disciplines, a fusion created by women of two very different temperaments. (Julie is an Idealist and Mary a Guardian.) This is not just a book on theory but a straightforward, hands-on "how-to"—a book designed to empower members of project teams to use new and creative ways to find and leverage synergies in their work preferences and to identify and compensate for conflicts in those same work preferences—and how to do all of this under the added stress of project deadlines.

Welcome to *Results by Design*. It is our hope that when you have completed this book you will have learned a little more about yourself and your fellow team members. We hope that you will feel empowered to make a real difference in the quality of your team's interpersonal dynamics and, as a result, make a positive difference in the outcome of your project.

Mary and Julia
October, 2004

Lessons from Geese

Based on the Work of Milton Olson

Fact 1: As each goose flaps its wings, it creates an "uplift" for the birds that follow. By flying in a V formation, the whole flock has a 71 percent greater flying range than if each bird flew alone.

Lesson 1: People who share a common direction and sense of community can get where they are going quicker and easier because they are traveling on the thrust of one another.

Fact 2: When a goose falls out of formation, it suddenly feels the drag and resistance of flying alone. It quickly moves back into formation to take advantage of the lifting power of the bird immediately in front of it.

Lesson 2: If we have as much sense as a goose, we stay in formation with those headed where we want to go. We are willing to accept their help and give our help to others.

Fact 3: When the lead goose tires, it rotates back into the formation and another goose flies to the point position.

Lesson 3: It pays to take turns doing the hard tasks and sharing leadership. As with geese, people are interdependent on each other's skills, capabilities, and unique arrangements of gifts, talents, and resources.

Fact 4: The geese flying in formation honk to encourage those up front to keep up their speed.

Lesson 4: We need to make sure our honking is encouragement. In groups where there is encouragement, the production is much greater. The power of encouragement (to stand by one's heart or core values and encourage the heart and core of others) is the quality of honking we seek.

Fact 5: When a goose gets sick, wounded, or shot down, two geese drop out of formation and follow it to the ground to help and protect it. They stay with it until it dies or is able to fly again. Then they join another formation or catch up with the flock.

Lesson 5: If we have as much sense as geese, we will stand by each other in difficult times as well as when we are strong.

Introduction

Imagine you are going to shoot a rocket to the moon. You don't simply point a rocket in the general direction of the moon and blast off, hoping for the best. Yet that is exactly how many projects are launched, with great surprise and amazement—and finger-pointing—when the target is missed.

There are, however, great similarities between a project and a rocket launch. That is not to say that it takes a rocket scientist to manage a project—it does not. However, a project destined for success has all of the attributes of a successful rocket mission:

- A clearly defined objective and a trajectory that defines the path from here to there
- An understanding of the things that can go wrong along the way, with plans to deal with them
- A plan for timely, relevant information to be passed within and between flight systems and flight control during flight
- Predefined parameters that identify expected levels of system performance during flight
- Regular monitoring of the progress of the flight, focused on key in-flight data
- The ability to compare actual performance against intended performance and to make midcourse flight corrections

There is one big difference between a rocket launched to the moon and a project, though.

A rocket is comprised of complex electronic systems—programmed and predictable in their behavior. These systems are prewired to work individually and together for optimal performance. By design, when an element in a system, or an entire system, runs below its expected level of performance, another compensates for it. If the compensation mechanisms fail, mission control can send override instructions, and the rocket will comply. It then continues on its path, almost effortlessly destined for its target.

Projects, however, are comprised of teams of people. Complex? Yes. They are undoubtedly programmed in their performance but hardly predictable in their behavior—if you lack an understanding of temperament (Keirsey, 1978, Berens, 1998). Project teams may seem designed to work at levels far removed from optimal performance, and no amount of orders from mission control—the project manager— may seem to make a difference. Many PMs fall victim to a disastrous leadership style: "There go my people. I must find out where they are going so that I can lead them." Project teams can seem hopelessly destined to fail, simply because they are made up of people with minds and wills—temperaments—of their own.

Yet it is exactly this diversity—a rich diversity of temperaments— that is the greatest asset of a project team. The project management process requires a breadth of capabilities and perspectives that simply do not exist in a single temperament.

Imagine a project team whose members not only follow the rigors of a robust project management process, but have also unlocked the mystery of how to maximize their work with each other throughout this process. Imagine a project team that works together seamlessly, "hard-wired" to work at optimal levels of performance, anticipating and compensating for each other's strengths and challenges every step of the way just like the complex systems of a rocket.

Fantasy? Not at all. Impossible? Absolutely not—as long as team members are willing to invest the time and the effort required to develop the necessary level of understanding of themselves and others, to develop the required plans, and to hold themselves (and each other) accountable to follow the project management process.

In this book we'll identify the steps of an elegantly simple yet effective and robust project management process and associated PM best practices. As we describe each step, we'll identify how each temperament relates to it and, at the same time, to other temperaments. We'll identify strategies to leverage synergies between the team members and how to avoid pitfalls.

This book can be used in many ways:

- By individuals, to better understand the dynamics of projects and project teams, and be more effective team members
- By project managers, to be more effective in managing projects

- By entire project teams, to be a step-by-step guide to enhancing project team performance
- By consultants, to provide a methodology to work with project teams to improve both team and project performance

The exercises in this book can be performed by either individuals or teams, allowing for self- and group-discovery.

This book can be especially useful as a step-by-step guide to kick off a project about to start:

- To frame and plan the effort by following a rigorous project management process
- To develop a team temperament profile and a team action plan for maximizing team performance.

This book can also be used to perform a project intervention, acting as a step-by-step guide for an in-depth assessment and as a planning tool for a project that is underway and in jeopardy. It can also be introduced at any point in any project to improve project and team performance.

From the Ground Up
Mission Planning

"It's kind of fun to do the impossible."
- Walt Disney

Overview of the Project Management Methodology

Mission Planning Synopsis— The Project Management Methodology

To many newly appointed project managers (and even some seasoned ones) the act of managing a project is daunting, and a formal project management methodology seems to be a series of disjointed activities that don't serve a larger purpose.

Simply stated, the goal of any project is to create some tangible object or some measurable condition (or a combination) that doesn't already exist: build a house, develop a software application, develop a fiscal budget, roll out new PCs to an organization, re-engineer a business. Some projects are outside of the realm of business: move a household from one location to another, plan and take an exotic vacation, remodel a kitchen—you get the idea.

Whether experienced PMs or not, we are all largely unconsciously competent in many aspects of project management. We don't think of certain everyday activities as project management, either in business or in our personal lives. Yet when a project is large—when the expected outcome is complex and fraught with risk, we tend to somehow think that to get it right, "there must be a trick to this." There isn't.

The same fundamental methodology works for any project: business or personal, technical or nontechnical, large or small. Although this book is not intended to be a course in project management, we do need a PM model to work from. What follows is an overview of a robust yet lightweight project management methodology. It can be applied by seasoned PMs as well as individuals new to the role of project management. We'll describe it in detail later and tie in the effects of temperament through each step of the process.

The Project Context

A project exists in a broader context as depicted in the graphic. Central to the project are its goals and objectives. While working to achieve those goals and objectives, management controls are placed around the effort. This is the project management methodology and will be the focus of our PM discussion in this book.

At the same time, it is important to recognize that other controls wrap around the PM methodology. Sometimes these other controls may exert a great influence on the project—and not always to the project's benefit. They are organizational methods and controls and customer methods and controls.

In a typical work environment, the project manager and the project team report to a line management team. If this organization holds any accountability for the success of a project, the line manager will typically use methods and controls of his or her own on the project: reporting requirements, status and issue management meetings, etc. The same is true of the customer; regardless the PM methodology in use by the project, the customer will likely have his or her own reporting requirements and meeting requirements.

To the extent that the project team communicates and executes a robust PM methodology, these additional layers of control may be minimized. The line manager and the customer may decide that the PM methodology employed meets their needs. However, it is often the

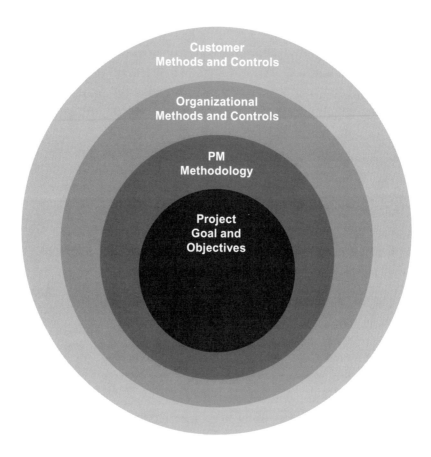

case that a project team is required to meet disparate and sometimes conflicting requirements of its own management and the customer. It is key to ensure that the core project management methodology is not compromised by these additional requirements, even if it means the PM must do some tasks twice. It's better to duplicate data in multiple different report formats (the Project Dashboard, used by the Project Team, one for line manager, and yet another for customer) than to set aside the Dashboard and lose sight of key project metrics. It's better to keep the core methodology intact and treat organizational and customer management requirements as an "upward pressure" to the management of the effort.

That context now defined, let's take a quick look at the project management methodology itself. We'll detail the methodology later in the book.

The Mission Profile: Defining the Project Scope and Creating the Project Plan

A project must have a purpose, and in PM terms this purpose is detailed through the project scope. The project scope answers three questions:

- What is to be done?
- When is it to be finished?
- How much will it cost?

The greater the detail specified in the "what," the greater the accuracy in the completion date and the cost.

Once these questions are answered, the next step is to create an overall plan to get from here to the desired outcome. If the desired goal is to build a house, for example, then a key part of the plan is to identify the steps to build a house with the characteristics and features identified in the scope. We call this the "scope-specific plan."

Note that we said the scope-specific plan is "a key part of the plan"—it isn't the only part. Failing to create and manage the other three subplans described below is a common mistake that project managers tend to make—even though on our own personal projects we identify and manage the other parts often without thinking about it.

A word about software development projects: The software development life cycle follows the same flow as the project management model presented here. In the area of scope, however, software projects go to great effort to identify software system requirements. These in-depth user and technical requirements are considered a part of the project scope and, as such, are also placed under change control. Methodologies to identify such requirements are beyond the scope of this book.

Flight Guidance Systems: Project Management Controls

Having a scope-specific project plan will get us only part way to the project goal. A robust project plan must take into consideration many other factors:

- What can go wrong and how to deal with it
- Who is involved in the effort and how to share information with them
- How the project team members will know that they're doing a good job in the eye of the customer
- How to deal with the customer's changes of mind

As a result, additional plans are required to augment the scope-specific plan:
- Risk management plan (identifies project risks and ways to deal with them)
- Communication plan (identifies stakeholders and how to exchange information with them)
- Quality plan (defines an acceptable level of quality and how to measure it along the way)

Each of these additional plans (risk, communication, quality) defines
- *who* (by skill or expertise, not by name)
- will do *what* (perform what task with a specific, tangible, and measurable outcome)
- by *when* (a specific date)

These plans are merged together to create an integrated project plan, and placed under change control. When we refer to "project plan" in this book, we are referring to this four-part, integrated plan. The project plan becomes the execution plan for the project team.

During the project life cycle it may seem that the only thing that remains constant is change: The customer changes his or her mind about the desired outcome. A member of the project team has a brilliant idea that saves a great deal of time, but requires an overhaul of the project plan. Management throws the project a curveball that risks the very success of the effort.

It is rare to have no change—by choice or by chance—during the execution of a project. However, change absent a degree of control is chaos—and introduces a significant risk of failure for any project. Defining and implementing a change control process is therefore critical to the success of a project.

Once the project manager knows what types of skilled individuals are needed, and for what time frames they are needed (as defined in the project plan), the PM then obtains the specific people (resources) for the project. The PM matches resources to tasks as appropriate and assigns people their duties. When the resources are readily available to the PM, this is a fairly simple task; however, when the necessary resources are outside the PM's control, risk and complexity are introduced into the project. We'll look at ways to identify and manage these situations.

Liftoff and In-Flight Control: Managing the Effort Underway

Once the planning is complete, the project team embarks on its journey. This execution time frame represents the bulk of the project life cycle and the phase where things typically unravel for a project.

The project manager is responsible for leading the team to success through myriad obstacles, keeping the team focused and the customer happy. Holding efficient and effective project status meetings is a critical success factor, as are effective risk management and timely and focused communications with all stakeholders.

Flight Tracking: Measuring and Reporting Results

While you are executing the project plan, you are at the same time measuring and reporting your progress against the plan. Selecting key performance metrics and displaying them on a "project dashboard" allows the PM, the project team, and the customer to see where they are against plan and, if they're straying off-course, allows them to identify and implement necessary changes to get back on target.

Onward to Re-entry and Touchdown:
The Cycle Continues

The project management process is an iterative cycle of identifying
your target, planning how to get there, and doing the necessary
work—while constantly monitoring and adjusting your plan as necessary. Just like a rocket in flight to the moon, a project is never static. It
is constantly in motion, subject to the forces around and within it.

Exercise

Think of some projects that you have worked on and answer the
following questions:

1. What was the best project you ever worked on? Why do you
   consider it the best?

2. What was the worst project you ever worked on? Why do you
   consider it the worst?

Overview of Temperament

2

Behind the Scenes of Human Interactions

Understanding temperament theory—the notion of how we are "hard-wired" to invoke certain cognitive processes—can help us establish a foundation for embracing and leveraging a diversity of personalities and talents. The ability to appreciate and engage different "cognitive strategies" provides us with an advantage over those who rely solely on traditional and well-worn linear thought. The ability to embrace our cognitive disparities has become an invaluable survival tool, particularly in today's fusion of enterprise and academia.

Knowing where to compete and how to collaborate is fundamental if organizations are going to survive and thrive in our new knowledge economy. It's no longer enough to merely be ahead of the competition. Breakthrough creativity, fresh ideas, and knowledge transfer are the new currencies. Our goal is to outthink and even outflank the competition by establishing a collaborative environment within our own domain.

Understanding Human Behavior

For the last twenty-five hundred years, "behavioral scientists" and psychologists have observed patterns of behavior that have been labeled or categorized to help researchers more easily organize and understand the human race. Recognizing, understanding, and embracing these behavioral idiosyncrasies can assist us in creating and nourishing a collaborative environment and in constituting the predictably superior team from which it invariably springs. Acknowledging temperament patterns and applying these insights to a team will facilitate clearer communication and increase productivity.

This integration of temperament and personality theory into twenty-first-century business practices often results in uniformly enhanced performance. Encouraging and enabling a collaborative blend of disparate individuals and complementary skill sets inevitably leads to observable and measurable differences in productivity and morale.

The behavioral models used here are simplifications, allowing the distillation of significant amounts of information into a usable tool. Simplifying many years of theory allows project managers to understand and use some fundamental principles without being students of psychology or behavioral technicians.

Human beings are complex adaptive systems possessing the ability to work outside any model we might fashion to explain human behavior. Environment plays an enormous role in determining who we are and how we act. Nevertheless, we have attempted here to provide a guideline to appreciate and understand the way we work.

In the next few pages we will be examining four temperament patterns that have been observed and examined by behaviorists for centuries. We will introduce you to exercises that will help determine your own "best fit" temperament and tune in to prospective team members' types as well. We'll relate these findings to the various components of the project management methodology, ultimately allowing you to leverage the diversity on your team.

The four temperaments express themselves individually, each with a very different core need that establishes the behavior of the organism.

The Artisan Approach

Tactical action epitomizes the Artisan approach. Often quick—seeking efficient solutions to get the project completed with the greatest impact.

Driven by the requirement for "freedom to improvise" or license to "act in the moment," Artisans fundamentally feel moved to make a visible impact on their world and people around them. Artisans continually scan their environment.

Artisans perform skillfully, priding themselves on accurately diagnosing the situation with which they are confronted, capitalizing upon available resources to address any urgency with agility and flexibility.

Artisans are contextual thinkers, often delivering fully functional results, that, incidentally, may not correspond to initial requirements.

Artisans thrive in rapidly-paced environments rich with variety and the opportunity to improvise, spurning long-winded and tedious political considerations. In both written and verbal communications, they believe less is more, being succinct to drive the message home.

Artisans have instinctive tool intelligence, with words often acting as their tools; their colloquial language is filled with sensory, vivid, action-oriented cues. Only when they are relating a story, weaving threads of complex data into a succinct whole, do they become verbose.

Stressors for the Artisan include mandated and seemingly endless planning and development processes. For Artisans, extended processes stifle energy and inhibit momentum; politics and process are their enemies. Planning, defining scope, and pondering process all appear antithetical to the Artisans' natural, psychological urge for speedy attack and conquer.

The Guardian Approach

An abiding concern for structure, process, and accountability exemplify the Guardian's approach to project management.

Dominant within their set of operational preferences, Guardians require defined goals and detailed objectives as descriptors for expected results. This requirement is dominant within their set of operational preferences.

Once armed with specific expectations, Guardians thrive on designing a route to the goal. Equipped with their detailed road map, specific parameters, and a responsible and serious attitude, Guardians are skilled at planning and considering contingencies on the way to their goal.

Guardians are also drawn to perform as caretakers, believing that team synergy and harmony are crucial to success. A grasp of both team and individual functions helps Guardians effectively balance and assign responsibilities among group members. Guardians are nourished by collegial and collaborative behavior, and disharmony or contention can threaten to derail the Guardian's train.

Another disruption can occur when sudden and gratuitous change is thrust upon the Guardian temperament. Guardians use past experience and accumulated skills as tools to craft intelligent and strategic solutions to project problems. Consequently, Guardians are more comfortable assuming customary roles and reaching for familiar goals.

Occasionally, Guardians undertake more than a reasonable share of the workload and, predictably, have difficulty refusing the additional responsibility. Notwithstanding the penchant to overextend themselves, Guardians can usually be depended upon to get the job done properly and on schedule.

The Rational Approach

Strategic focus is central to the Rational's method of managing a project.

Competence, mastery of technique and control over circumstance are cornerstones of the Rational psyche. Both logic and analysis comfort and equip Rationals, helping them with a view toward the longer term, the broader horizon, and the entire scope of the task at hand.

Rationals are driven to assess the "whole," and from that perspective they are adept at evaluating areas of competence, with a goal of perfecting the system.

Rationals have a talent for choosing people for their team, seeking confirmed expertise in both obvious and associated areas. They leverage knowledge management and make informed choices, including content knowledge experts wherever possible.

Rationals believe that projects—as systems—are organic, self-regulating, and, consequently, self-developing.

Possessed of a healthy skepticism, Rationals presume most endeavors, including their own, to be rife with error.

The efficiency and effectiveness component is always present within the Rational mind-set. Rationals prize strategic intellect highly and often abandon task specifics in favor of delivering results on time and on target.

Often pedantic and long-winded, Rationals are typically calm and reasoned. Intrigued by a challenge that engages them cerebrally, Rationals enjoy a debate and can argue either side of an issue with equal facility.

The act of being forced to deliver an unrefined result will often fracture the Rational's composure, and contending with a faulty or poorly designed process that the Rational cannot improve upon will generally obscure the Rational's view of the finish line.

The Idealist Approach

Relationships are at the center of an Idealist's life. Creating meaningful connections with others is what drives Idealists. Both passion and vision motivate and inspire these energetic and voluble communicators.

Equipped with an extraordinary ability to sense authenticity, Idealists are frequently skilled diplomats, able to mediate, negotiate, and proselytize on behalf of their project or team. An undeniable empathy helps them open traditionally closed channels of understanding, building bridges not only connecting the team members but improving their understanding of project goals as well.

Kindness, harmony, and purpose are mandatory prerequisites to properly ignite and inspire Idealists. But once recruited, Idealists will tirelessly and intelligently devote themselves to a project.

Idealists are skilled motivators, and their sincerity and enthusiasm can be a powerful means of influencing group behavior, especially if the perceived result of the project will be life enhancing. Collaborating with others to create a significant result is fulfilling to Idealists.

Able to recruit or enlist less-gifted or uncertain individuals, Idealists often inspire people to attempt what was once considered impossible.

Occasionally, Idealists will hire people with "potential" rather than currently demonstrated skill. In doing so, Idealists can become overly involved with people, inadvertently abrogating the responsibility of delivering project results.

In the interest of avoiding conflict, Idealists can tend to be inappropriately accommodating, the result of which can be a problematic and fatally compromised end result.

The Temperament Context

According to widely recognized temperament theory, most healthy individuals are driven by a need to "psychologically survive."

It is thought that individual identifiable temperaments are motivated by very fundamental needs. When those core needs are not being met, it is common for most individuals to display symptoms of psychological starvation, or stress. Reacting instinctively, many individuals remain unconscious about the unique and definitive temperamental issues that dictate their behaviors.

As individuals begin noticing the recurring patterns or themes with which they deal during the course of their lives, the specific visible behaviors that correspond to stress points will usually provide clues to some of our most deeply felt internal musings. Developing an awareness of our own core needs is fundamental to any exploration of our temperament and psychological makeup.

Visible (observable) behaviors manifested by each temperament—as successive stages of the project management process are dealt with—will correlate to temperament categories. However, caution is advised in arriving at preliminary judgments about yourself or others, especially when relying upon an insufficient sample of observable behaviors.

The Temperament Context*

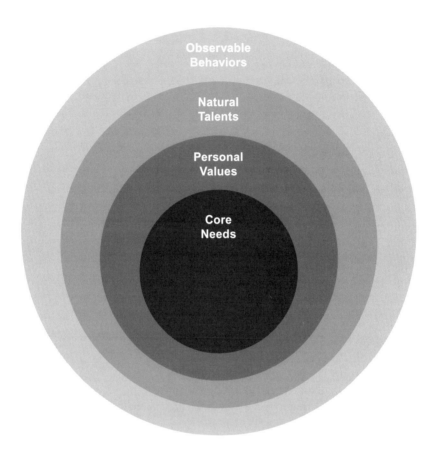

*Concept, graphic, and labels taken from *The Temperament Targets*™, Linda V. Berens, *Understanding Yourself and Others®: An Introduction to Temperament 2.0* (Huntington Beach, Calif.: Telos Publications, 2000)

Here's an example of temperament being misdiagnosed for an air traffic controller:

The job description demands being completely present, highly attuned to the environment, fast paced, and able to make split-second decisions. If you observed someone in that job, you might conclude from the observable behaviors that he or she is of the Artisan temperament.

While the tactical Artisan temperament would have natural talents for this type of position, the other three temperaments could also perform the job. But they might do it as a result of very different core needs. Artisans might be attracted to air traffic control because it provides freedom to act in the moment, to be tactical, to make an impact, and it is exciting and fact paced.

Guardians might be attracted to air traffic control because they enjoy the extraordinary responsibility, the presence of an established process, the safekeeping aspect, and the notion of belonging to a large community that is in service on a national and global level.

Rationals might be attracted to air traffic control because of the complex systems in use and the ability to participate in driving worldwide travel and commerce. There may be the opportunity to improve the system and gain expertise in a very crucial and specialized area.

For Idealists, air traffic control provides the ability to express their commitment to making the world a smaller or more inti-mate place, increasing the understanding between nations resulting from international travel. Idealists' commitment to connecting people to one another affords the incentive to deal with the daily stresses of an air traffic controller's envi-ronment.

Let's examine the core needs and values of each temperament and how they can influence, but not limit, behaviors.

Artisans

Core needs:
- Freedom to act contextually
- No constraints
- Making an impact
- Attention
- Concrete, tangible results
- Having options available

Values in a team environment:
- "Play before work" mind-set
- Fast pace
- Skillful performance
- Quick minds
- Communication essence, short-hand
- No lies or exaggeration
- Fundamental understanding of function and position
- Team working like a well-oiled machine
- Risk takers
- Results

Talents on a team:
- Acute attention to sensory data
- Aesthetics
- Superior execution
- Action orientation
- Transforming intangible data into tangible product
- Tool intelligence
- Understanding of the way things work
- Political savvy, ability to be blunt
- Ability to figure out a way to remove or circumvent obstacles
- Efficiency
- Ability to tolerate lack of structure
- Enjoyment of variety
- Tactical intelligence

Stressors for Artisans:
- Too much structure
- Boring project
- Redundant tasks
- Step-by-step process
- Insufficient or improper tools to accomplish task
- Ignoring people's contributions
- Inability to make an impact
- Lack of demonstrable progress
- Restrictive environment

Artisan mantra: Just do it...now!

Guardians

Core needs:
- Respect
- Benevolence
- Belonging to a group/community/team
- Tradition
- Honor
- Trust

Values in a team environment:
- "Work before play" mind-set
- Balanced workload
- Formal reporting structure
- Clear roles and responsibilities
- Clear objective or intended result
- Working together harmoniously as a team
- Valuing all contributions from team members
- Limiting possible risks
- Plans and contingency plans

Talents on a team:
- Industriousness
- Hard workers
- Process orientation
- Responsibleness
- Organizational strength
- Detail orientation
- Follow through
- Disciplined
- Efficiency and effectiveness
- Planners
- Keepers of tribal knowledge
- Understanding of what has worked historically
- Avoiding unnecessary risks
- Installing safeguards
- Affinity for structure
- Including all team members
- Helpfulness
- Creating clear processes
- Logistical intelligence

Stressors for Guardians:
- Lack of structure or clear process
- Change for change's sake
- Change without merit
- Team members not carrying their share of the workload
- People not adhering to the process
- Lack of hierarchy
- No stability or security
- Sloppy work
- Irresponsibility
- No objectives/goals or clear delineation of tasks

Guardian mantra: Efficiency, Effectiveness, and Community

Rationals

Core needs:
- Competence
- Mastery
- Independence
- Control over destiny
- Expertise

Values in a team environment:
- "Work is play" mind-set
- Working only with domain experts
- Working autonomously for the group
- Opportunity to improve or develop a system
- Discovering truths
- Complex problem solving
- Research
- Intellectual inquiry and rigor
- Debate over diverse ideas

Talents on a team:
- Enaging the "right" people for the team
- Depth of knowledge
- Wisdom
- Substantiated evidence and proof for assertions
- Precision in word and deed
- Strategic intelligence
- Future focus
- Logical decision making
- System thinkers

Stressors for Rationals:
- Incompetence
- Being made to look foolish
- Public humiliation
- Overly emotional team members
- Subjective decision making
- Not having all the information
- Being perceived as ridiculous objectives
- Working on the parts rather then the whole
- Minutia

Rational mantra: Universal principles and universal truth

"Here where I Reside"

Idealists

Core needs:
- Meaningful work
- Unique contributions
- Significance
- Quality of relationships
- Depth of connection with others

Values in a team environment:
- Personal relationships
- Causes that they believe in
- Championing for the rights of people
- Harmonious working relationships
- Working for a common goal
- Objectives that forward the human condition
- Opportunities to grow and develop themselves and others
- Trust
- Congruency in word and deed
- "Work is meaning" mind-set

Talents on a team:
- Diplomatic intelligence
- Deep understanding about people
- Ability to connect people
- Building bridges between disparate points of view
- Collaboration
- Enthusiasm
- Generosity
- Ability to connect with people on a very deep level
- Engendering trust
- Creating open and honest environment
- Catalyst
- Seeing people's potential even if they don't see it
- Communicators on a very visceral, authentic level

Stressors for Idealists:
- Cold, aloof people
- No communication
- Thoughtlessness
- No appreciation
- People overlooking their intellect due to their people focus
- Naysayers
- People who won't cooperate with their ideas
- Too much logic
- Not taking the people aspect into consideration
- Working on a project that doesn't matter
- Working in isolation
- Not valuing or acknowledging their contributions

Idealist mantra: Heart, soul, intention

Exercise:

What do you think is your "best fit" temperament?

What is your second best?

What temperaments are you certain that you are not?

In general, how would someone close to you describe you?

Mission Profile
Know Where
You're Headed

*"If you do not know where you are going,
any road will get you nowhere."*
—Henry Kissinger

Project Failure
and Project Critical
Success Factors

3

Payload Integration:
Integrating Temperament Theory into
Project Management Methodology

Before we attempt to identify the steps to project success, it is
important to first perform triage on project failure. According to
the Standish Group, which studied IT software application projects,
almost one-third (31.1 percent) of all such projects were cancelled
before they were completed. Over half of these projects (52.7 percent)
cost almost double (189 percent) their original estimates.

Less than 20 percent (16.2 percent) of all projects were completed
on time and within budget. (In the largest companies, this figure
dropped to an abysmal 9 percent.) Of the few projects that were
completed on time and within budget, which is not to imply that they
were "successful," on average, less than half of their originally scoped
features were ultimately delivered.

Projects rarely fail because either the project manager or the project team did not know how to manage the project. The fundamental

project management process is well understood and well documented and has changed little over the last twenty years. Companies regularly train their staff on PM methodologies, develop their own standardized PM methodologies, and many even certify their project managers through robust programs such as the one offered by PMI (Project Management Institute).

Intellectually speaking, managing a project is easy. A project manager simply follows mature methodologies to:

- define scope and deliverables, including agreed-upon price and delivery date
- create and manage according to a project plan
- identify and manage issues and risks
- identify and implement quality standards
- identify and communicate with key stakeholders
- manage requests for change

Why, then, do projects fail?

First, let's look at what a failed project means. Any project has four key variables: scope, budget, delivery time, and quality. A failed project is one in which the client perceives an unanticipated shortcoming in one or more of these areas.

Note that success is not in the eyes of the project team. The client will ultimately determine a project's success or failure. For example, a project whose scope falls short of client expectations does not have all the features or functionality that the client expected. Ramifications of such perceived shortcomings can be significant: a black mark in someone's performance appraisal, refusal to pay for work done, or in a worst-case scenario, litigation.

That is not to say that a project is successful only when it concludes per the originally agreed-upon parameters of scope, budget, time to delivery, and quality. Quite the contrary—change is the constant companion of every project, as any project manager will readily attest. Even the most successful of projects can encounter dramatic changes through the project life cycle.

What distinguishes the successful project from the failed one is that at every step along the way, the project manager, the project team, the management hierarchy, and the customer are always "on the same page." If a project involves multiple partners in the delivery process, such as vendors who are subcontracting in the effort, count them in as well.

A successful project is an effort whose extended membership acts as one, constantly driving toward and supporting all members to achieve a well-understood and commonly held goal, dealing with the inevitable issues and changes with confidence, integrity, and a dogged determination to find win-win outcomes when (not "if") difficulties arise.

Successful projects are the result of balanced skill, execution, and discipline in three areas:

- Technical expertise: The domain-specific expert-level skills required to deliver on the project scope. If the project is to build a house, then technical expertise is that expertise required to build a house—including architecture, plumbing, roofing, and so on, and the discipline to apply that expertise.
- Conceptual expertise: Knowledge of, and experience in, a mature project management process and the discipline to follow that process.
- Human expertise: Knowledge of, and experience in, human interactions in project teams under stress and the discipline to use it.

Note that these skills and disciplines are required of the entire team—not just the project manager. Not that every member of a project team needs to be an expert in all three domains of expertise; rather, each member of the team must fully understand his or her primary area of technical expertise and at the same time have a working knowledge of fundamental principals of both project management and human interactions.

All team members need to understand the project management process so they can contribute appropriately and fully as the project progresses, minimizing risk and maximizing team performance. In successful projects, all team members follow the same PM methodology and are disciplined in their joint execution. Everyone understands the project and plays by the same rules.

Likewise, all team members should understand temperament—their own, their colleagues', and the best ways to interact among the various team temperaments—so that they can contribute appropriately and fully as the project progresses, minimizing risk and maximizing team performance. Again, everyone plays by the same rules.

Like a three-legged stool, if a project team falls short in any one of these areas, project execution will be unbalanced, and the effort will be at significant risk of failure.

The Standish Group identifies the following as the top three critical success factors for projects:

- User involvement
- Executive management support
- Clear statement of requirements

Exercise

Think of various project teams you've worked on, worked with, or encountered. What examples of failed projects can you think of? What happened? What was the cause of their failure?

- Lack of technical expertise/discipline?
- Lack of conceptual (PM) expertise/discipline?
- Lack of human expertise/discipline?

If you believe the cause of project failure was outside these areas, explain why.

The underlying skills required to achieve these critical success factors rely on the ability to communicate effectively with customers, management, and other team members. Effective communication requires great facility with human expertise: the ability to exchange information fully, openly, and honestly; without ambiguity; and often under difficult circumstances.

Although great emphasis (training, certification, assessment) is placed on technical and project management expertise, little attention, if any, is placed on human expertise, yet it is a critical success factor for project execution.

To maximize project success, project managers, project teams, and even customers need first to understand each other at the personal level: their styles, strengths, challenges, and work preferences.

In many projects, it is not the PM process that fails but an individual's or team's ability to deal with the human challenges that surface during various stages of the PM process. By looking at the project management process through the lens of temperament, we can see individuals' strengths and challenges throughout the PM life cycle, help teams find creative and innovative ways to leverage each other's strengths, and avoid exposing the project to the risks of each other's weaknesses. Through this integrated, holistic approach we can better understand and prevent the underlying causes of project failure.

In the following section, we'll detail the steps of our project management methodology and discuss the strengths and weaknesses of the various temperaments for each project step. Technical expertise is beyond the scope of this book.

Project Goals
and Objectives

4

Why Does This Project Exist in the First Place?

Any project begins with a goal. Here are some examples:

- To develop and deploy a new customer order tracking software system
- To improve call center performance
- To develop next year's fiscal budget
- To build a retirement home

The goal is then broken down into objectives. These objectives place the goal into a specific context, putting quantifiable measures and time frames around it. Using call center performance improvement as an example, some objectives might be as follows:

- Increase call volume by 5 percent by June 1, without adding call center agents.
- Decrease call wait time by an average of twenty seconds by June 1.
- Decrease call abandon rate by 10 percent by August 1.

• Increase call center agent retention by 20 percent by September 1.

Together, these objectives make the goal very clear to all parties. They also can help to identify the financial and business value of achieving the goal. This financial gain, in combination with the cost of the effort to achieve the goal (derived from the integrated project plan), creates an ROI (return on investment) model for the effort.

Project managers and project teams are most often given the project goal and objectives as the starting point for their effort. When project team members are provided only a goal for their effort, it is key for the team to develop objectives and get the buy-in of key stakeholders prior to beginning the effort. If stakeholders are not aligned on the objectives, the project is at great risk of failure. How could any project succeed if team members are asked to hit a target they can't see or, worse yet, asked to hit multiple, conflicting targets?

PM Best Practices

• Have a clearly defined goal for your project, supported by a series of measurable, time-bounded objectives.

• Ensure that all key stakeholders are aligned in their support of the project's goal and objectives. If they are not aligned and in support, address the issues immediately.

Project Scope

5

Let's start with an exercise.

Scope Exercise 1: My Dream Home

Think of your dream home. Imagine that you are about to speak
with the architect/builder who will lead the project to build it. Identify
everything you think should be included in the project scope. Put this
description aside and save it for later.

As you recall, the project scope answers the following questions:
- What is to be done?   (Content)
- When is it to be finished?   (Time frame)
- How much will it cost?   (Budget)

Content breaks down into three categories:
- Features and/or requirements: What are the required characteristics or features of the end product?
- Constraints: What limitations might affect the end product?
- Quality Objectives: How will we know and/or measure how well a job is being done?

In any project, there needs to be a careful balance among the content, time frame, and budget. They are closely coupled, and changes to any one will affect the others. If the content is the driving force of the customer, then it will dictate time frame and budget—the more content-rich the effort, the more expensive it will be and the longer it will take to complete. If the budget is the driving force, then content will have to be closely managed—to keep costs down, the customer will have to forego the "bells and whistles." At other times, the time frame is fixed and can't be moved.

Regardless the prevailing force of the project scope, scope definition is not complete until all components are defined.

The following sample framework is a simple way of capturing a project scope. A blank framework may be found in the appendix.

Scope Definition Framework

Project Name: Retirement Home

Project Manager: Pulte Homes / Jo

Budget ($): $200,000.00

Budget Resources (Staff Hours):

Due Date: 06/01/2002

Project Goal:
To build a unique, custom, luxury retirement home on a lot that the client already owns.

> The goal should be specific, measurable, and actionable.

> Consistency check all aspects of project against the others. Identify and eliminate inconsistencies:
> - Too feature rich for budget or due date?
> - Unrealistic constraints for budget or due date?
> - Stated features inconsistent with goal?

Major Features:
- 3 bedrooms
- 2,000 square feet
- Open and airy feeling
- Great room (kitchen/family roo
- Elegant simplicity—not ornate
- Kitchen sized and laid out for 4 s
- Kitchen to have view of garden
- Library not really a 3rd bedroom

> "Open the box" on your customer's thinking through open-ended questions. What the customer says he or she wants may not be what the customer needs.

Project Constraints:
- Local building code
- Odd shape of lot
- Homeowners association aesthetics guidelines
- Height restrictions
- Must be handicap accessible

> Constraints often impact budget and delivery date. Make sure they are identified proactively, not discovered accidentally.

Quality Assessment:
- Pass all building code inspections
- Pass homeowners association reviews
- Schedule owner walk-throughs and sign-offs
- Have no major punch list items
- Receive certificate of occupancy

> Proactively identify the steps that will be taken to ensure quality, as well as how quality will be measured.

> You will manage according to dollars, resources, or both.

Scope Exercise 2: Return to Your Dream Home

Return to your dream home scope description from the prior exercise. Cast the information into the scope definition framework. Note the areas you may have neglected to consider. Update your scope description.

PM Best Practice:

- Don't worry whether any specific item is a feature, a constraint, or a quality indicator. As long as you have thorough discussions with your customer and identify and document everything that will guide or affect the Project, it doesn't matter.

Integration Checkpoint: Project Scope and Temperament

6

As with each step in the PM process, each temperament comes to scope definition from a different perspective. Defining a scope requires developing very specific details (certainly more details than you had time to develop in your brief exercise) so that the project team can determine the cost and delivery time frame. Some temperaments are more comfortable doing this than others. And there can be great value in having a multitemperament team define the scope.

Temperaments will show themselves in what people say and do. Following is a summary of what you may hear and see from different temperaments during scope definition:

Artisans and Scope Definition

What Artisans may likely say:
- "What does this matter? It's all gonna change."
- "It depends."
- "Let me play devil's advocate."
- "Give me the gist."

What Artisans may likely do:
- Get impatient: fidget, tune out
- Shift attention to their agenda
- Jump to quick-and-dirty solutions
- Feign interest

Key Artisan strengths in this phase:
- A creative eye for "quick wins"
- Keen insight into tactical possibilities

Key Artisan challenge in this phase:
- Refrain from jumping into execution

Guardians and Scope Definition

What Guardians may likely say:
- "Can you be more specific/exact/precise?"
- "Let's start with…" (implying structure and order)
- "And what about you?"
- "What will it look like when we're done?"

What Guardians may likely do:
- Stay very focused on the topic
- Start to create structure and order
- Draw visuals
- Be very engaged and animated—be involved

Key Guardian strengths in this phase:
- An orderly, thorough discovery process
- An early perspective on future logistical needs

Key Guardian challenge in this phase:
- Give others room to be (and think) less organized

Rationals and Scope Definition

What Rationals may likely say:
- "Why?"
- "Let's look at the big picture."
- "Can you be more specific/exact/precise?"
- "Can you clarify…?"

What Rationals may likely do:
- Stick to a point until people demonstrate a thorough understanding
- Use (and request) very precise language
- Be reflective and thoughtful—pause while they think things through
- Strive to improve the outcome—drawing distinctions and using a process of elimination for that which does not fit the model

Key Rational strengths in this phase:
- Creating a well-considered model for the final outcome
- Long-term focus

Key Rational challenge in this phase:
- Visualize an outcome that they are invested in but may not match the customer's vision

Idealists and Scope Definition

What Idealists may likely say:
- "How do you feel about…?
- "That's great…" (reinforcing positives)
- "What about (other involved people)?"
- "I know this is a tangent, but…"

What Idealists may likely do:
- Become "angel's advocate"
- Think big—broaden the possibilities
- Inspire people—see potential for people
- Create buy-in across the team and stakeholders, drawing parallels and threads of meaning using a process of integration to find ways to make all perspectives fit

Key Idealist strengths in this phase:
- Diplomacy
- Identifying and involving all key stakeholders

Key Idealist challenge in this phase:
- Try to integrate all ideas—even though they may not create a consistent model or system

Exercise: Go to the Case Study Project Team

What might be the synergies between team members during scope definition? Challenges?

Who might find scope definition easy? Difficult?

Creating A Scope-Specific Project Plan

7

You will recall that every project has a goal and a set of objectives, and now it also has a scope—a description of the set of features and functionality of the end product, what the product will look and feel like to the customer. The next step in project planning is to create the scope-specific plan.

It would be impossible to address domain-specific plans in the context of a book—there are too many possibilities: software development, financial planning and management, business process design and re-engineering, and many more. Nonetheless, we can cover some basics to help ensure the scope-specific plan is robust.

If objectives further refine the project goal, then activities and tasks drill down to even greater levels of detail and make the project actionable.

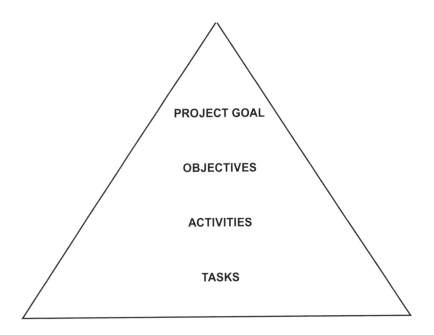

Each objective can be described by one or more outcomes that are required to meet the goal. In our earlier call center example, our goal was to improve call center performance. To achieve that goal, we defined several objectives, one of which was to increase call center agent retention by 20 percent by september 1. We can launch several activities to achieve that objective:

- Conduct (the currently late) performance reviews.
- Perform (the currently late) salary reviews.
- Increase the size of call center agents' cubicles.
- Investigate the possibility of call center agents telecommuting and taking calls from home.
- Create a call center agent board of directors to gain ongoing input and insight from the agents.

Let's say, after thorough discussions with key stakeholders, including the agents themselves, we decide to do all of these. Although these are all great ideas, none of them are actionable in their current state. Even further breakdown is necessary to transform these activities into tasks—discrete, actionable items that would be the line-item components of a scope-specific plan.

Taking the first activity as an example, a series of tasks is required to conduct performance reviews. In the following list, each task is described in terms of who is going to do what by when. At this point, you may know only the organization that will perform the work, not the individual. That's fine—we'll obtain the individual's name later in the project.

- Send memo to all agents about performance plan process and dates by May 15. (Corporate Communications)
- Distribute performance input forms to all agents by June 1. (HR)
- Hold Q&A session with agents by June 5. (HR and call center managers)
- Agents to provide self-evaluation by June 15. (Call center agents)
- Call center managers to evaluate Agents by June 15. (Call center managers)
- Agent/manager one-on-one meetings to be held to discuss individual performance by July 1. (Call center managers to call meetings, agents to attend)
- Final performance evaluations complete by August 1. (Call center managers)

Some of these tasks are autonomous—they stand alone and can be done at any point prior to the September 1 date set in the objective.

Others are interdependent and either precede or succeed other tasks in serial fashion. It is important to understand and define these relationships between tasks so you can determine what activities can be performed in parallel and which must be performed in serial. To optimize your scope-specific plan and ensure you are driving to the ultimate goal in as efficient a manner as possible, challenge yourself to maximize the number of parallel tasks—within the constraints of resources and cost.

Once you have broken down every objective to its set of activities and tasks, you now have the information you need to create the Scope-Specific Plan. This plan can be placed in Microsoft Project or any other project management tool. The use of such tools is beyond the scope of this book.

PM Best Practices:

- Break down the project objectives to activities and tasks, and enter them into the project plan.
- Ensure each activity and task directly supports the goal and objectives. If one does not, then question if it belongs in the project plan.

Flight Guidance Systems

Planning for the Unexpected

*"Every minutes spent in planning
will save two in execution."*
—Henry Kaiser

Risk Management

8

We now know what our goals and objectives are and have identified the activities and tasks that are required to achieve the goal. But as we've discussed, other factors are at play that need attention. Additional plans and project controls are needed to ensure that we are successful.

Guidance System Alpha:
Creating a Risk Management Plan

The goal of risk management is first to identify what might go wrong and then to take steps to make sure it doesn't. This is called risk avoidance. But project teams can't always control everything—some risks are unavoidable. What you can do in that case is identify steps to minimize the impact to the project. This is called risk mitigation.

As the project team assesses risk, it is important to focus efforts on those risks that not only are most likely to occur but also would have the greatest negative impact on the project. Project teams can go overboard managing risk by mounting risk avoidance and mitigation efforts for every risk identified. It is key that project team members focus their limited resources on those activities with the highest payback. In the case of managing risk, this means that teams should identify how likely a risk is to become a reality and identify the probable outcome and its relative impact on the project. Only high-likelihood, high-impact risks warrant action.

The following framework identifies a structured thought process for project risk management.

Risk Management Framework

No.	Risk	Likelihood	Risk Outcomes	Impact	Mitigators Avoid/Minimize	Reasses Date
1	Carpenters Union Local 1275 will go on strike on February 1	High	Construction delayed Client unhappy Lose weather window	High	Avoid: See if Carpenters Union 176 plans to support strike—if not, work with union Minimize: Arrange non-union labor Tell client about risk Communicate with union to stay on top of status	January 15
2	Rainy season will last longer than expected	Medium	Delay in landscaping	Low	Avoid: None Minimize: Tell client about risk Ensure landscaper can work around any delay	March 1
3						
4						
5						
6						

Transform any high-likelihood, high-impact risks into action plans—either add them to the project plan or place them on an action item list.

Some risks are simply out of your control—you can do nothing to avoid them. Ensure you have a plan to stay on top of them and identify steps to minimize the risk if it should occur.

Although this framework facilitates a structured discussion of risk, the identification of risk avoidance or mitigation steps alone does not complete the work necessary to create an actionable risk management plan. Until you have identified who will do what by when, you do not have an actionable plan. Many teams stop once potential, theoretical risk management plans have been identified. The missing step is to transform high-likelihood, high-impact risks into actions. By assigning the risk avoidance and/or mitigation steps to individuals and by assigning due dates, a project team ensures that the necessary steps will be taken and that there will be no ambiguity about who is to take them.

Risk Management Exercise:

Develop a risk management plan for your project (or if more appropriate, the case study). You will find a blank framework in the appendix. When you are done, answer the following. How easy was it to complete the plan?

- Did you dive right in or did you mentally "check out"?
- Did you have trouble thinking of any risks?
- Did you identify more risks than you expected?
- How easily did you identify avoidance and mitigation plans?
- On a scale of 1 to 10 (10 being high), what is your tolerance for risk? Why?

Integration Checkpoint: Risk Management and Temperament

9

Let's look at how the four temperaments relate to risk management.

Artisans and Risk Management

Artisan tolerance of project risk:
High: Artisans trust their skillful performance in any situation

What Artisans may likely say:
- "Don't worry about it."
- "We'll figure it out when we get there."
- "Risk? What risk? That'll never happen."
- "We're wasting our time—we have work to do."

What Artisans may likely do:
- Get impatient: fidget, tune out, play class clown
- Feign interest
- "Stir the pot"
- Underplay risks, trust their own ability

Key Artisan strength in this stage:
- Identify the "players" and political risks

Key Artisan challenge in this stage:
- Refrain from jumping into execution

Guardians and Risk Management

Guardian tolerance of project risk:
  Low: Guardians tend to be pessimistic, fatalistic

What Guardians may likely say:
  - "Wow, there's a lot that can go wrong."
  - "What if…?"
  - "You know, the last time I did this…"
  - "We should/ought to…"

What Guardians may likely do:
  - Identify a great number of risks
  - Make contingency plans (and plans for plans)
  - Appear pessimistic (but they're really not)
  - Make very conservative (negative) assumptions

Key Guardian strength in this stage:
  - Identify risks to budget, time, and scope

Key Guardian challenge in this stage:
  - Overstating and overmanaging risks

Rationals and Risk Management

Rational tolerance of project risk:
  Variable: tolerance depends on the degree to which Rationals trust the competence level of the team

What Rationals may likely say:
  - "What are the underlying reasons for risk?"
  - "If this happens ... then we can expect…"
  - "Where do we need to end up?"
  - "Who has the expertise to accomplish this?"

What Rationals may likely do:
  - Design a new system to integrate the risk
  - Be naturally adept at impact mapping
  - Critique the risk
  - Logically weigh pros and cons

Key Rational strength in this stage:
  - Identify risks around necessary skills/expertise

Key Rational challenge in this stage:
- Worrying about risks to their model rather than risks to delivery

Idealists and Risk Management

Idealist tolerance of project risk:
High: Idealists are optimistic and trust in good outcomes

What Idealists may likely say:
- "Don't worry about it."
- "Okay, let's try it."
- "Risk? Are you sure we can't mitigate it?"
- "I'm sure it will all turn out fine."

What Idealists may likely do:
- Overpromise and (at times) underdeliver
- Make sure everyone's okay
- Underplay risks in order to gain buy-in
- Engage in consensus-driven decision making

Key Idealist strength in this stage:
- Identify risks to alignment of ideas and values

Key Idealist challenge in this stage:
- Not saying yes to everything—being practical about what can/can't be done

Risks and Issues:
A Closer Relationship Than You May Think

Projects often have separate mechanisms for managing risks and managing issues. Unfortunately, that often creates confusion for team members and tempts them to shift their energies—after all, issues are real and need to be addressed. Or do they?

When we assess risks, we focus energy only on those that are high likelihood, high impact to ensure we apply our limited project resources to those activities with the highest payback. If you think about it, an issue is simply a risk that has become a reality. Its likelihood is 100 percent—higher than high—it's there at that moment, staring you in the face. But just because something has become real doesn't mean you have to do anything about it. In the case of a risk that is high likelihood but low or medium impact, the team will take no immediate action—although they will keep track of it in case the impact to the project changes over time. The same is true of issues.

An issue may have been already identified as a risk on your risk management plan, but this is not always the case. Issues can material-ize out of the blue, despite the best planning and insights of project teams. When this occurs, it is key to follow the same thought process as if it had been already identified as a risk—identify its impact to the project and take action only when the impact is high.

Customers often identify "issues" and demand that project teams take action to address them. Often this is no more than a well-intentioned reaction when robust risk and issue management is not in place. Rather than let a customer decide how to expend a project's resources by declaring something an issue, take the customer through the risk and issue management thought process.

For any "issues" customers identify, have the customers describe the outcome in tangible terms and assess the impact to the project. They will often realize that although there is an "issue," it isn't critical and need not have resources re-assigned from other tasks to address it. In those cases where customers have identified a high-impact issue, they have done the project and the project team a great favor. Includ-ing customers and even third parties in risk and issue management allows teams to have a robust, 360-degree view.

Risks and Assumptions:
How to Go from Passive to Active

Most projects are rife with assumptions. Don't know something for a fact? Make an assumption. Look at any project documentation and you'll no doubt see a lengthy section on assumptions. Assumptions are a powerful tool to place your project plan into a larger context. They show the project's "mind-set" and the thought process used to arrive at the plan and risks.

Yet assumptions can and do backfire. Many projects that have deliverables to be provided by third parties "assume" that all deliverables will be made on time and with quality. How often does an assumption of this nature turn out to be true? Not very often. Then what? Project plans that make assumptions like this have little or no wiggle room built in to deal with the outcome. But even if they do, they've already missed the highest payback approach to dealing with the situation.

Using the example above, that a third party will deliver on time and with quality, we can convert this assumption to a risk. There is a risk that the third party will not deliver on time or with quality. Let's say the likelihood of this is high—the vendor in question has a poor track record of deliveries to you. Further, let's say that the impact to the project is high—the deliverables are in the critical path of the project timeline, and the project would suffer a day-for-day slip for each day of delay from the vendor.

We now have a risk with a high-likelihood and high-impact: it's time to develop a risk management plan to avoid the risk if possible or, if not, to mitigate the impact of the outcome. With just that simple shift in perspective, we've gone from passively making a poor assumption to proactively managing a situation that risks the success of the project. Challenge each of your assumptions and turn them into risks. What is the risk to the project if your assumption is wrong? What steps can you take to increase the likelihood that your assumption is true?

Does that mean a project should never have any assumptions— that they all should be converted to risks instead? No. Having a list of assumptions is a powerful contractual tool. Assumptions provide protection to your project—a safety valve of sorts—when the best made (and proactively managed) assumptions turn out to be wrong. Continue to maintain a list of project assumptions, and in addition, convert each to a risk and follow the risk management methodology. Once you have a chance to look at your risk management plan for your assumptions, you may choose to drop some from your assumptions list and place them instead on your risk management plan, especially if they are low likelihood, low impact.

With an eye toward documenting meaningful assumptions, keep those that are high-likelihood, high-impact risks on your list of assumptions. These are the areas where you need both the protection of documented assumptions and at the same time the proactive approach of managing the risks around them.

PM Best Practices:

- Transform risk management plans into unambiguous actions (who/what/when) for high-likelihood, high-impact risks. Add these actions to either your project plan or your project action item list.
- Include the entire team (customer, third parties, etc.) In the identification and management of risks.
- Revisit risks throughout the project—the risk landscape may change dramatically over time, especially as the project encounters changes to the scope.
- Take both issues and assumptions through the risk management framework. Issues are simply risks that have become a reality, and assumptions are often project risks in disguise.

Communication
Management

10

Why spend time communicating when there's so much work to do? When asked why they communicate on the job, most people respond, "To provide information." It certainly doesn't seem to be a high-payback activity. Yet scratch the surface of this response by asking this question: Why do we provide information?

We typically communicate in business to get action. Whether the action is immediate or deferred, we want people to act in a way that supports our project, and we communicate with them to provide the necessary information to do so. We want and need

- the customer to provide complete requirements
- executives to support the project and provide interference when needed
- third parties to deliver what we specify when we need it
- project team members to deliver to a common set of deliverables and time frames

What often seems to be little more than providing innocuous information is really setting the stage for some future action that supports the project's ultimate success. Or, perhaps better stated, it should be setting the stage. If the groundwork is not properly laid, the ultimate action required by a key stakeholder for the project to succeed may never materialize. Worse yet, the project may create its own risks and issues by falling into one of the following communication traps:

- Overcommunicating (too much information, wrong set of stakeholders)
- Undercommunicating (too much work to do to "waste" time on communication)
- Miscommunicating (mixed messages, vocabulary mismatch)

A communication plan ensures that the project reaches out to key constituencies with targeted messages that facilitate the actions needed by the project. Developing a communication plan begins by identifying the project stakeholders. They become the target audience of your communications. Among potential stakeholders are the following:

- The customer
- The project team
- Suppliers/subcontractors
- Partners

Even within each of these stakeholder groups, there may be other constituencies:

- Team members
- Management
- Executives
- Individuals/groups affected by the project

Effective communication is a two-way exercise. One-way communication (like corporate e-mail) guarantees neither that the recipients will read it nor, even if they do, that they'll respond. The goal of developing and executing a communication plan is to facilitate the exchange of information between you and your intended recipients. Key message "sound bites" should be carefully crafted in advance and used consistently when communicating through various media. Lead with two-way communication and followup, underscore, and reinforce key points with one-way communication. Ensure that your communication plan allows for sufficient one-way and two-way communication.

The following annotated framework demonstrates how a project team can develop a communication plan.

Communication Management Framework

Put yourself in your customer's shoes: what would you want to hear, and when would you want to hear it?

Proactive communication increases customer satisfaction.

Task	Target Audience	Messages	Rationale	Communication Channel	Assigned To	Due Date, Trigger, or Frequency
1	Customer: Mr. and Mrs. Doe	Status of house building Show pictures of progress	Anticipate questions and alleviate concerns by being proactive.	Meet in person (once a month) Meet by phone (remainder) Progress pictures through e-mail	Project Manager	Weekly (Mondays)
2	Construction Team	Upcoming weeks' targets Prior weeks' successes	Keep team motivated and focused on progress Get early read on potential problems.	Construction team beer bash	Construction Supervisor	Weekly (Fridays)
3	Customer: Mr. and Mrs. Doe	Achievement of major project milestones	Celebrate milestones	Phone call (as milestones occur) Display plaque (with all milestones —present at completion)	Project Manager	Per scheduled project milestones
4	Vendors	Advance notice of anticipated shipment of materials: confirm date and materials ordered.	Minimize possibility of problems and/or delays	Phone call	Construction Supervisor	3 weeks prior to scheduled ship dates
5						

Be creative—look for ways to encourage communication among team members even as you deliver key messages to them.

Don't forget to treat partners and vendors as members of your project team. Your success rests on their ability to succeed. Provide them the knowledge they need to be successful.

Who are your stakeholders?

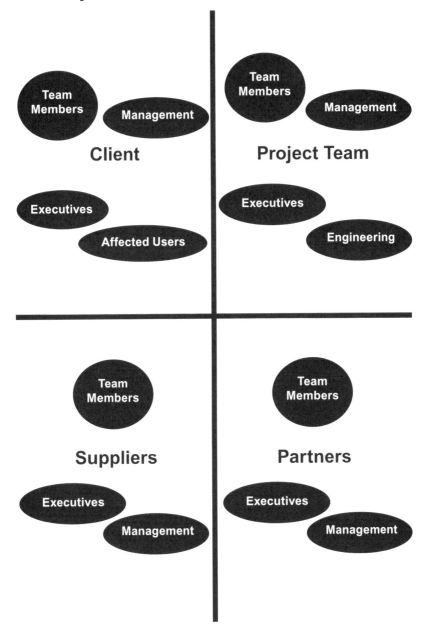

Communication Planning Exercise:

Develop a communication plan for your current project (or for the case study if you have no current project.) You will find a blank framework in the appendix. When you are done, answer the following. How easy was it to develop the plan? What are your observations?

Integration Checkpoint: Communication Management and Temperament

11

How each temperament communicates is unique. Consider the following aspects of communication for each temperament:

Artisans and Communication

- Use concrete data and similes
- Are tactical and to the point: net it out
- Use colloquial and concise language
- Use casual body language
- Use physical humor to make an impact
- Are clued in to other people's motives
- Communicate to get the job done

Guardians and Communication

- Use concrete data
- Are linear and sequential
- Use traditional language, are respectful
- Use formal body language
- Use sarcastic, dry humor
- Want to understand relevant experience
- Develop relationships through communication

Rationals and Communication

- Use abstractions: theories and concepts
- Are strategic
- Use precise language, exact wording to describe the nuance of an idea
- May seem distant and preoccupied
- Use cerebral humor, double entendres, puns
- Strive to understand underlying principles, and expect competence in others
- See communication as a forum for intellectual query

Idealists and Communication

- Use abstractions: people and needs
- Are thematic
- Use exaggeration and generalization, analogies and metaphors
- May appear warm, gushing
- Use self-deprecating jokes
- Want to understand importance to others
- Use "global" language words like "always," "never," "forever"
- Communicate to learn more about people

PM Best Practices:

- Don't neglect to communicate—the degree to which you communicate will determine the ultimate success of your project in the eyes of your customer and/or your management.
- Communicate to all customer stakeholder groups—ensure your customer's management and executives hear your story, not someone else's version of it.

Communication Exercise:

Revisit your communication plan. Identify how others might perceive the communication style of each temperament. What might be some possible communication style conflicts? What combinations of communication styles might lead to misunderstandings?

(If you used the case study for the last exercise, continue to use the case study project team.)

Quality Planning

12

Quality isn't guaranteed in any project—no matter how diligently the project team works. It takes a determined, proactive approach to ensure that the result of any project will be a set of outcomes that the customer considers to be of true quality. After all, the customer will be the ultimate judge of your work. Yet ask a PM or project team how to ensure quality and you'll get dramatically different responses.

Since quality is "in the eyes of the beholder," then it is crucial to literally get your customer's eyes on the work product—as early and as often as possible—during the course of the project. If you attempt to engage your customer in a discussion of quality early in the project, he or she may respond, "I can't describe it to you, but I'll know it when I see it." So show your customer your product early in the life cycle (even if it's simply a mock-up or sketchy user interface), and continue to show it often as the project progresses.

Although project teams blanch at the thought of showing a customer less than the final product—there are bugs that need to be worked out, after all!—customers are typically eager to be involved.

Customer inspection, early and often, fosters open two-way communication and helps keep everyone on the same page. Involving your customer will help uncover "hidden requirements," miscommunications, and project planning errors. Customer involvement minimizes the risk of "surprises" late in a project where the only recourse is to spend more time and money to address them (i.e., Fix them.)

Some simple steps that can be taken to assure quality include the following:

- Show the customer mock-ups of project outputs as early as possible.
- Have the customer review interim deliverables.
- Involve the customer in project testing at appropriate points.

In each of these cases, it is key to have the customer "sign off" the activity—documenting not only that the customer was a part of the process, but that he or she agrees to and accepts the results.

Following is a sample quality management framework.

Quality Management Framework

Quality Objectives:

- Pass building code inspections on first inspection
- Pass home owners association aesthetics inspection
- Hold customer building-in-progress walkthroughs (4) on schedule
- Resolve all in-scope customer-identified items to customer's satisfaction
- Have no major punch list items at final acceptance walkthrough

> *Quality objectives should be specific, measurable, and achievable. The inspections identified below are the steps that will be taken.*

Internal Inspections:

- Construction supervisor walkthroughs
- Project manager audits

> *Challenge yourself and your project team to find ways to self-inspect. Make time for these inspections, and include them as milestones.*

External / Customer Inspections:

- Customer building-in-progress walkthroughs (4)
- Homeowners association aesthetics inspection
- Building code inspections

> *Ensure your customer has opportunities for inspection as well—preferably multiple opportunities. Head off any discrepancies between what the customer expects and what you plan to deliver—ASAP.*

Integration Checkpoint: Quality Planning and Temperament

13

Absent a quality plan that creates concrete inspection points for assessing quality, each temperament will view the quality of the project from his or her own unique perspective. Although a quality plan is able to provide points of inspection and facilitate a dialogue with the customer, each temperament will still impose a personal vision of "quality" onto other dimensions of the project: the project process and the team process. By creating a quality plan, teams are able to minimize the interference of team member temperaments with the customer's own definition of quality.

Yet as we look at these other dimensions of quality—the project process and the team process—through the lens of temperament, we discover that quality has dramatically different meanings to individual temperament types, as well as the external customer.

To a Guardian, quality is about process:

- Following logical, orderly, and traditionally successful steps to achieve a result will ensure a positive outcome.
- For optimal performance, the team should follow the logical, orderly, and

deliberate steps employing a disciplined fashion. This process will help detail clear and reasonable expectations from all team members.

To an Artisan, quality is about "impact":

- Shortcuts are a great way to quickly achieve a positive outcome while finishing the project; they also provide plenty of time to amend or append whatever might need fixing.
- Inspired spontaneity generally leads to optimal team performance while accommodating the constantly shifting landscape and promoting individual and team innovation.

To a Rational, quality is about perfection:

- Designing an intellectually perfect model or system guarantees a positive outcome.
- Team members should hold themselves—and one another—to extraordinarily high standards of performance. This will intellectually challenge team members, encouraging them to continually learn, thus gaining competence and mastery.

To an Idealist, quality is about interpersonal interactions:

- Customers and team members who feel good about themselves and each other usually achieve positive outcomes.
- Team members should appreciate the unique talents of one another; working toward the "greater good," even at the expense of self-sacrifice. This selfless stand encourages the team to deliver results far beyond what they dreamed possible.

PM Best Practices:

- Show your customer your work product early in the project life cycle and often throughout the project.
- Have the customer sign off on the project quality plan and all quality inspections.
- Don't worry whether an item should be categorized as a requirement, a constraint, or a quality target. At the end of the day it doesn't matter, as long as the topic is discussed, commitments are documented and signed off, and you deliver to it.

Exercise:

Identify the fallacies of each of the "quality truths" for each temperament.

Which statements resonate with you? Why?

Which statements seem ridiculous to you? Why?

Change Control

14

Once a project's scope and plan are defined and baselined, all elements of scope, budget, deliverables and due dates, and quality are placed under change control. This allows a project team to have a fixed target to drive the project toward at any point in time. Yet project teams typically encounter compelling reasons to change a project over the life of the effort. This change must be managed effectively, or a project can spiral out of control.

By using change control, a PM can formally welcome requests for change. Prior to accepting them, team members can research their impacts to the project—whether a change is initiated by the customer or suggested by a team member. A meaningful dialogue, and often a hearty negotiation, can occur between the project team and the customer during the assessment of a requested change. This quality dialogue ensures that all the necessary information is uncovered and communicated before a change is incorporated, and the project's direction is shifted.

Without change control, a project is at risk of "scope creep," a common dilemma for project teams. Whether instigated by a customer or a well-intentioned team member, additional features and functionality may be added to a project over time. Without a formal mechanism to understand the potential risks and impacts of these additions, projects slowly but surely increase in scope, yet the due date and budget remain as originally defined. A lack of change control usually results in due date slips, quality problems, and budget overruns.

A change control framework facilitates the process of requesting, assessing, and responding to change requests.

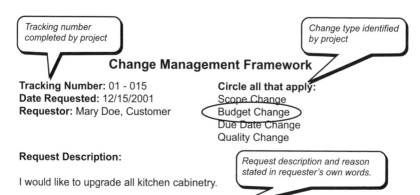

Change Management Framework

Tracking Number: 01 - 015
Date Requested: 12/15/2001
Requestor: Mary Doe, Customer

Circle all that apply:
Scope Change
Budget Change
Due Date Change
Quality Change

Request Description:

I would like to upgrade all kitchen cabinetry.

Reason for Request:

Samples submitted for my review were not acceptable. I do not expect to have to pay more than was originally quoted.

Project Analysis/Recommendation: **Date Submitted:** 12/20/2001

Tried new cabinet vendor for this job—promised better quality, lower prices. That did not prove to be the case. After discussion with the customer, reverted to old vendor. Samples from old vendor are acceptable to the customer. Agreed to split the cost differential with customer. Total budget uplift: $9,000.

Agreed Changes:

Scope: No change.

Budget: Overall budget increase of $9,000. Cost to be split between project and customer. Project budget is now set at $209,000. Cost billed to customer now set at $204,500.

Due Date: No change

Quality: No change

_____   _____
Requester Signature / Date   **Project Manager Signature / Date**

If the mere volume of work to be done within the scope of the project creates stress for team members, then adding a measure of change to the environment "turns the heat up" even more. We've already looked at how the temperaments react when under stress— let's now look at how the temperaments respond to changes to the project under stress.

PM Best Practices:
- Revisit all other aspects of the scope when there is a requested change to one. Because they are all so highly inter-related, you can't change one without anticipating a change to the rest.
- Revisit both the risk management plan and the communica-tion plan at every change to the scope.

Exercise:
Think of a time when you were making great progress toward a goal and you were faced with a change of plan or direction. What was the situation? How did you react? Why?

Integration Checkpoint: Change Control and Temperament

15

Change under stress evokes different reactions from the various temperaments than do their typical stressors. If you go back and review the typical stressors for the temperaments, you will see that these stressors are caused by a certain perception on the part of the individual—the actual situation may or may not be real. (Although you could argue that if the individual perceives something to be real, then it is real.)

But in the case of change, there is no doubt—a change request is real, and its generation is outside your control. You are at the mercy of the customer, who seems to be constantly changing his or her mind. You are duty bound to take each request seriously, analyze it, and make a well-balanced recommendation. And, by the way, you are expected to do this on top of everything else you and the rest of the team are doing—in your copious spare time.

Change: more stress, less control. How do the temperaments react now?

Change Management and Temperament

Temperament	Will typically agree to change when:	Knee-jerk reaction to change request under stress	Motivator	When dealing with change under stress, may appear:
Guardian	Analysis is complete and the plan and process are updated	Will deny the need for (or value of) change	Doesn't want to change "the plan" and put the project at risk	Rigid
Artisan	It's fun and competitive or the opportunity to shine is seen	Will make consideration for any change	Enjoys challenge, fun, excitement, variety	Reckless
Rational	The change has been researched and is believed to be logical and consistent with model or system	Will intellectualize the change and attempt to fit it into the system or model—but will move more slowly due to stress	Wants to ensure the integrity of the model or system and the quality of the result	Overly analytical
Idealist	All points of view have been integrated and everyone is satisfied	Will agree to change prior to analysis—then will agree with the team that change is inappropriate	Desires harmony— wants to please both customer and the project team	Wishy-washy

Resource Management

16

The biggest challenge for every temperament is having the nerve to proceed with less than every resource identified as necessary to the project. Rarely does a project team have carte blanche to obtain everything identified—unlimited access to money, people, information, and so on.

However, to even have a hope of maximizing the resources available to the project, once identified, you have to ask for them. That means you run the risk that someone might respond, "No. Period."

What now?

Anyone can ask for what he or she needs to get the job done. But sometimes requests must be made under very difficult circumstances. Here are just a few examples:

- If you get the desired resource, another key project will be put in jeopardy.
- The resource (team member) you need is already working sixty or more hours a week.

- You know the resources don't exist (money, people, etc.), but the project team has identified them as critical to the project's success.

Exercise:

What do you do when you can't get something (or someone) you need to perform a job you're held accountable for? How does it feel?

Integration Checkpoint: Resource Management and Temperament

17

Let's look at what motivates the various temperaments to put forward those particularly difficult or awkward requests and how they respond when they receive a no as the answer.

Regardless the reaction, at the end of the day, project teams will often need to move forward with less-than-desired resourcing levels. When this occurs, teams rarely have the option of waiting until the resources are available—business typically mandates that they move forward as best they can.

When project teams must move forward with fewer resources than they deem necessary, it is key to employ risk management and communication management. What are the risks to the project and the outcome if we proceed without these resources? Once risks and mitigation plans are identified, who needs to be made aware of these risks? In this way, the PM process supports itself and allows progress to be made even under less-than-ideal circumstances.

Resource Requests/Constraints and Temperament

Temperament	Makes requests most readily:	When told no, typical response takes the form of:	If the answer is still no, (creating a perceived crisis), may:
Guardian	If he or she believes it is his or her duty or responsibility	- Logical argument (if-then-else—impact on project) - Qualitative argument (impact on team harmony)	Be tenacious—keep trying to get to yes and at the same time identify/manage risks
Artisan	When he or she sees what's in it for him or her	- Logical argument (if-then-else—impact on organization) - Qualitative argument (impact on lost opportunity)	Jump into crisis management mode
Rational	Only when it increases the quality of the result	- Logical argument (if-then-else—impact on model or system) - Qualitative argument (impact on relative perfection of model or system)	Fall into "analysis paralysis"
Idealist	If it is in people's best interest	- Logical argument (if-then-else—impact on team) - Qualitative argument (impact on individual team member)	Have an emotional reaction

In-Flight
Tracking and Control
Navigation Tools

*"Don't be afraid to take a big step when one is indicated.
You can't cross a chasm in two small steps."*
—David Lloyd George

Effective Project
Status Meetings

18

Once the project is launched, everyone is busy working. Meetings may seem like constant intrusions on progress, and there's always a crisis lurking around the next corner. Project teams typically operate under tight deadlines, with a constant gray cloud of stress overhead.

Stress takes its toll on individuals and teams in the heat of project execution. For projects to be successful, team members must pull together and work even more cohesively during stressful periods. Yet it is exactly at these times that the diversity of temperaments among the team can pull the team apart and jeopardize the very success of the project—each temperament poking at the "buttons" of another.

Each member of the team must take personal responsibility to do everything possible to keep this from happening. And team members do want to avoid a "team implosion." But how can they?

First, we'll look at holding efficient and effective project status meetings—key to ensuring that team members spend the maximum time on the work they need to perform for the success of the project.

We'll then look at temperaments under stress and provide teams with clues for identifying behaviors under stress and how to deal with them.

Effective Project Status Meetings

Exercise:

If you could have it your way, how would meetings be run? Identify your pet peeves and propose "best practices." (Feel free to identify "worst practices," too!)

At the heart of every efficient and effective meeting is an agenda. An agenda identifies:

- the meeting's purpose
- what is to be discussed
- the expected outcome(s) of the discussion (enumerating key decisions to be made, if any, in advance)
- how long the discussion will last
- who will lead (facilitate, control, referee) the discussion

Many meetings follow this format but still degrade into long, tortuous affairs. Have you been to a meeting where

- there were unrealistic expectations about how long a discussion would take?
- the wrong people were in the room to make a decision?
- no one was "facilitating" the discussion—and the discussion got out of control?
- a short project status meeting ended up being a long problem-solving session?
- two people had a long conversation that was of interest to no one else in the room?

Here are four simple guidelines that, when implemented, can transform project status meetings into focused, high-leverage forums:

- Recognize that project status meetings are to discuss the project status against the project plan.
  - Status is articulated as on target, at risk, or past due. If a deliverable is at risk or past due, succinctly identify the containment plan, due date, and owner.
  - Status meetings are not to be used to provide a blow-by-blow description of what happened since the last meeting.

- If a new issue has surfaced, identify it, the owner, and the projected closure date. Do not engage in a detailed issue discussion. If one is necessary, hold a separate meeting.

- Invite only decision makers, or their fully empowered delegates, to attend project status meetings.
    - One (and only one) decision maker per area may participate in the discussion.
    - Others may attend as silent observers.
    - If there is not a quorum of decision makers/delegates, reschedule the meeting.

- Identify an active meeting facilitator.
    - Track the time—keep the discussion on assigned time targets.
    - Track the discussion content—keep the discussion on target and moving forward.

- Keep and review an action item list. (See Appendix A for an example.)
    - Clearly identify actions: who/what/by when.
    - Do not skimp on action item descriptions. Write in complete sentences and include what the output is expected to be. Do not write just a quick phrase, thinking, "Everyone will remember what this means." Everyone won't.
    - Track and succinctly document the project status. The action item list is a living document and a valuable project artifact for either new team members or for historical purposes.

Integration Checkpoint: Stress and Temperament

19

Exercise:

What are your stress triggers? How do you behave under stress?

Each temperament has a unique set of stress triggers and typical patterns of behavior under stress that are visible to others. The challenge is for team members to see the behavior patterns of a team member under stress, point them out, and help the team member move beyond the situation. No one behaves well under stress, and no one performs his or her best under stress. It is in the best interest of team members, as well as project success, to deal directly and openly with stress.

Stress and Temperament

Temperament	Typical stress triggers	Normal (nonstress) response	Under stress may appear to	Caricature stress quote
Guardian	- Not feeling part of the group - Someone not carrying his or her weight - Not following the process - Uncertainty	- Fix the process - Rally the team	- complain - blame - micromanage - worry and/or nag	"But we didn't plan to do it that way."
Artisan	- Feeling constrained - Lack of freedom - Lack of tools for the task at hand - Boredom	- Work around the system - "Stir the pot"	- retaliate - sabotage - compete - blackmail	"I'll see you one, and I'll raise you one."
Rational	- Feeling incompetent - Lack of knowledge - Lack of self-control - Too many variables - Information imbalance	- Seek expertise	- suffer "analysis paralysis" - obsess - be robotic - nitpick	"I could have been masterful, if only…"
Idealist	- Insincerity - Betrayal - Lack of integrity - Lack of recognition	- Work to improve the relationship	- avoid the issue - fake "all is well" - "freeze or frenzy" - get depressed	"Everything is just wonderful!"

Exercise:

Review the temperament stressors. How might some temperaments inadvertently create stressful situations for others?

What might you be able to do to help keep your personal stress level in check during a project life cycle?

"Houston, we have a problem..."

20

Imagine a group of people—adults and children—on a boat on a large lake. A child wanders too close to the edge of the boat and falls overboard. The following is a caricature of the possible reactions of the various temperaments:

- **Artisans:** Instantaneously toss their drink, kick off their shoes, and dive into the water to save the child.
- **Guardians:** Recall what they learned in lifesaving class. The first thing one should do is…
- **Rationals:** Assess and mentally redesign the safety systems on the boat to prevent a similar incident in the future
- **Idealists:** Console the child's mother and reach out to others in distress over the situation.

All temperaments work well in their areas of specialty during project execution. When crises occur—and they inevitably do—each temperament will do his or her best in the situation, consistent with the person's level of technical expertise and true to the temperament's tendencies. In crisis, though, it is the Artisan who often comes to center stage.

Throughout the planning cycle, we've seen Artisans challenged and frustrated by the rigor and discipline—and time—required to develop a robust project plan. Their bias is action, and only once they are doing something will they truly be in their comfort zone. Add a healthy dose of impossible odds, and Artisans will be in top form.

The Artisan is often the hero of the project crisis—asserting leadership and expertise, rallying the team, finding a solution quickly (often "quick-and-dirty"), and driving the crisis to closure.

But don't ask the Artisan to perform a root-cause analysis or implement a process and procedure to ensure the crisis will not happen again. The Artisan either has returned to work or has moved on to address the next project crisis.

In general, look to the Rational to determine the failure of the model or system, the Guardian to find and fix failures in team process, and the Idealist to ensure that the team members retain a sense of common purpose and to smooth over any interpersonal "rough edges" that may have been a result of the crisis.

See how it truly takes all temperaments to achieve optimal team performance?

It is critical to focus on defining the actions that will get the project back on target. Although reflection on "what went wrong" is a necessary part of process and performance improvement, it is not wise to perform a postmortem in the heat of the moment. First, determine how to get the project back on track and put those plans in motion. Once the project is at, or near, the desired state, assemble a team to review the situation: perform a root-cause analysis, identify errors or omissions in the process or approach that was used, and make the necessary improvements. Do not use a postmortem as an opportunity to blame an individual. Even if someone did do "something stupid," a system or process failure let the person get away with it.

A Word about "Be Like Me" Syndrome*

When projects are high-stress, fast-moving initiatives, we all want to fall back on the familiar and operate in our own comfort zones. Through the lens of temperament, this means we try to find people who work the same way we do. To the extent that we can surround ourselves with individuals of similar work styles—similar temperaments—we can seemingly communicate in shorthand, if we even need to communicate at all. To an outsider looking in, it may seem that the entire process is telepathic. We feel safe; we feel comfortable.

When people work differently than we do, we may try-- under stress—to force them to fit our model, to "Be Like Me." It is exactly when we attempt to force our style—our temperament—on others that problems arise. This can manifest itself in many ways. Following are just a couple of examples. Be Like Me can manifest itself as

- the Guardian PM micro-managing an Artisan
- an Idealist PM expecting a Rational to think that it's okay to go ahead without complete scope definition—"We'll get there over time, and besides, the customer is happy with what has been identified to date."
- an Artisan PM telling the team that there is no time to do risk management, so the team shouldn't bother bringing up any risks—"Just deal with them if they should arise."

*Berens, 1998. Originally identified by Dr. Sue A. Cooper.

As you've seen by now, the individuals on the receiving end of such directions will be extremely uncomfortable and will attempt to find ways to remove the discomfort and get back to safe, familiar territory. The PMs, on the other hand, are trying to deal with stress by creating a team of people who work just like they do. The results can be disastrous.

Fire Prevention versus the "Arsonist Firefighter"

The overarching goal of any PM methodology is to ensure success through thorough planning: create a plan, minimize surprises, and remain in control of events. Absent a robust PM methodology, projects often encounter otherwise avoidable crises. This can lead to the creation of a "hero culture" on the project, as team members (particularly Artisans), rise to meet each crisis with great energy, ingenuity, and sense of purpose.

Life in a hero culture can be a very heady experience. Such projects are often fast paced, highly competitive, intellectually stimulating, and electrically charged with a sense of self-importance. In a hero culture, you literally never know what might come next, but you'll be ready for it—and you'll typically be rewarded generously for your heroic efforts.

Unfortunately, these rewards are self-defeating. A project team with a hero culture is not motivated to do a rigorous job of planning and, in effect, creates most of its own crises. The very energy, ingenuity, and sense of purpose that a hero culture expends on crisis resolution, if spent on robust planning, would lead to a greater degree of project success.

PM Best Practices:

- Use the project plan and the project action item list as the project road map. These two documents alone should be able to provide all tactical direction necessary for the team.
- Don't shoot the messenger: when a crisis occurs, listen, question, plan, and act. Perform a retrospective postmortem only after the crisis is resolved.

Project Dashboard

21

As project team members are executing the project plan, they have
status meetings and report on their results. A "project dashboard" is a
tool that can be used to display key project metrics, showing current
performance and trends. the dashboard is divided into four quadrants,
showing key metrics for scope, schedule, budget, and quality—the
dashboard contents should derive directly from the scope template,
the quality plan, and the project plan. A dashboard is key to quickly
identifying where a project stands relative to its objectives. Exception
conditions can be quickly noted and containment plans identified.

It is very easy to focus on budget and schedule—they are the
stuff of common management practice. Scope and quality are often
challenging to measure and track, though.

As we've seen, scope creep can jeopardize a project. Unchecked,
scope creep can manifest itself in slips in deliverables; a deliverable
grows in size and complexity when it is subject to scope creep. Absent
insight into how much change is occurring to the scope, and how
effectively a team is dealing with it, due dates can be missed and the

customer can become very unhappy—even when he or she is the one initiating the changes. By tracking the scope on a project dashboard, the project team has a leading indicator for schedule—if the scope is under control, the schedule should not be at risk. Conversely, if the scope is being bombarded by constant change requests, the schedule is at great risk—and so is the budget if the customer chooses to withhold payment until deliverables are met.

Just as scope management is a leading indicator for schedule, quality is a leading indicator for budget. The customer holds the ultimate power in the definition of quality. If the customer does not believe the project has delivered quality, the customer can—and often does—refuse to pay. By tracking quality milestones on the dashboard, the project team can rest assured that quality discussions are occurring and that the customer is signing off along the way. When a project team delivers a final product with no prior discussions regarding quality, all team members hold their breath while they await the customer's final verdict on the quality of the delivery—not a good position to be in when payment for the effort hangs in the balance.

It is critical to focus reporting on a small number of key project metrics. Projects and customers often fall prey to micro-managing their own efforts by widening the field of measurements to track and analyze. This typically accomplishes little more than adding overhead to the project efforts. At its worst, though, the practice can send projects spiraling out of control through a continual series of course changes triggered by micro-managing minutiae.

A project dashboard is intended to show the current state of the project and provide insight into future performance through extrapolation and trend analysis. It is not intended to be a measurement tool for individual team member performance.

Project Dashboard Framework

Project Name: Retire...
Project Manager:
Due Date: 06/01/02
Dashboard Date: 01/01/02

Budget ($): $200,000
Resources (Staff Hours):

Scope:

	# Change Reqs Submitted	Number Approved	Number Declined	Number Pending	% On Time Responses
This period	5	0	4	1	80%
Last period	15	3	6	6	15
Project to date	43	25	17	1	43

> Large numbers of change requests imply that either the customer is attempting "scope creep" or requirements were inadequate.

Budget: (...oped ...eded)

	Actual to Date	Future Spending	Project Total	Budget	Variance
This period	55,412	150,000	205,412	200,000	5,412
Last period	43,797	150,000	193,797	200,000	(6,203)
	167,520			200,000	(32,480)

> This trend shows some unanticipated startup costs. It's time to get matters under control.

Schedule:

	Target	Actual or Projected	Status
Major Milestones:			
1. Design Architecture	12/01/01	12/01/01	GREEN
2. Break Ground	01/15/02	01/30/02P	RED
3. Complete Framing	03/01/02	03/01/02P	YELLOW
4. Exterior Complete	04/15/02	04/15/02P	GREEN
5. Interior Complete	05/15/02	04/01/02P	GREEN
Major Deliverables:			
1. Architecture Blueprts	12/02/01	12/02/01	GREEN
2. Detail kitchen design	01/31/02	01/31/02P	GREEN
3. Detail bath design	02/15/02	02/15/02P	GREEN
4. Landscape design	03/01/02	03/01/02P	GREEN
5.			

> This confirms some startup problems. But it looks like the schedule might be salvaged by the next milestone. Set customer expectations.

Quality Objectives:

	Target	Actual or Projected	Status
All Inspections:			
1. Pass Code Inspections	PASS	02/25/02 02/25/02P	GREEN
2. Pass HOA Inspection	PASS	03/15/02 03/15/02P	GREEN
3. Customer Walkthrus (3)	On sched	03/20/02 03/20/02P	GREEN
4. In-scope changes	Satisfactry	03/25/02 03/25/02P	GREEN
5. No major punch items	No major	04/01/02 04/01/02P	GREEN

PM Best Practices:

- Derive the contents of the project dashboard from the scope template, the quality plan, and the project plan. If the customer or management requests different items on the dashboard, ensure that such a request doesn't constitute a change to the Scope of the effort. If the request does represent a change to the scope, follow the project change control process.

Flight Commander Profile

Who's Driving...and What's Driving Them

"One definition of Leadership is the ability to recognize the special abilities and limitations of others, combined with the capacity to fit each one into a job where he will do best."
—Unknown

The Role of the
Project Manager

22

The role of the PM is a cornerstone in the project team. The project manager is the team's leader, whether that function is formalized in the organization or not. As the leader, the PM has an incredible influence on the team—both in terms of the project management process the PM chooses to follow (or not) and in terms of the environment he or she creates for the team.

Some organizations mistakenly assign the PM role a strictly administrative function—creating and editing the project plan, tracking action items, and so on. When this happens, it only means that someone else is acting as the de facto project manager; Whether by caveat or chance, another person takes leadership responsibilities for the project. At best, it might work—once everyone has "figured out" what's going on and assuming that the de facto PM has all the necessary skills and influence. Far more frequently, though, it is a death knell for the project: no one is "in charge," the project flails as competing interests try to drive the project direction, and the customer loses confidence in either the project manager or the project team.

We'll look at the role of the project manager from three perspectives:
- Project managers and temperament-influenced leadership styles
- Project managers and temperament-influenced communication styles
- The paradox of the "perfect" project manager

Temperament-Influenced Leadership Styles

Assuming that the project manager leads the project team through a documented and well-understood project management process (such as the one presented in this book), the project team has a clear structure to work within. But as the PM and the team make their way through the process, the leadership temperament of the PM will always show through—and be exaggerated under stress. Absent a formalized project management process (obviously not recommended!), the leadership temperament of the PM will dictate the PM process.

As we've already seen, the four temperaments have clear ways of approaching both work and other people. Let's now look at how the temperaments influence our leadership styles.

Artisan

Values
Flexibility, freedom, fun, and ability to make an impact

Typical leadership tendencies
Hands off

Under stress, leadership style may be perceived as
Unpredictable and impulsive. Under stress, Artisan PMs may take unnecessary risks for the excitement and challenge of having to deal with them and for the opportunity to do what they know they do best—handle a crisis. They may appear to be purposefully sabotaging the project. They can become uncooperative with anyone who will not go along with their agenda, whether it's a team member or the customer.

Best approach to use when PM is under stress
Don't hem in Artisan PMs. Present them with options. To move Artisan PMs in the direction you hope for, create a challenge (even make it a competitive challenge) to spur them to rise to the occasion. They'll go into action when given a meaty challenge. If structure is needed, create it for the team, but don't impose it on Artisan PMs—they won't accept it.

Guardian

Values
Structure, process, order, rules, hierarchy, closure, and action

Typical leadership tendencies
Well organized, predictable, process-oriented, and action oriented

Under stress, leadership style may be perceived as
Dictatorial and dogmatic. Under stress, Guardian PMs will retreat to the comfort of structure and order, believing that through these alone the project can be successful. But Guardian PMs will also more strongly assert their place at the top of the project hierarchy and become overly focused on the need for closure and action—and driving both, under extreme stress, with or without the support of the team.

Best approach to use when PM is under stress
Follow the Guardian PMs' rules. If you take issue with the rules, do not violate them—discuss them privately with Guardian PMs and use logical (if-then-else) arguments, focusing on the impact to the project and/or the team. Reach an agreement—and stick to it. Focus on your deliverables and action items. Communicate status against these proactively and often. If you have issues, raise them only after briefing the Guardian PM on your status.

Rational

Values
Expertise, competence,continual improvement of skills and abilities, and well-thought-out, logical solution models or systems

Typical leadership tendencies
Strategic and future focused; will model a solution, then backwards engineer to determine appropriate approach

Under stress, leadership style may be perceived as
Arrogant and critical. Under stress, Rational PMs may become disengaged with execution details, leaving them entirely to the team. Becoming hyper-critical, Rational PMs may become argumentative and unforgiving. In extreme cases, they may suffer analysis paralysis and become unable to execute fully in their role.

Best approach to use when PM is under stress
Bring solutions and supporting evidence to Rational PMs—prove your assertions using logic. Frame the situation, and ask what Rational PMs think—give them the opportunity to demonstrate (to themselves as much as to you) that they are experts whose opinion are valuable. Never imply or infer that Rational PMs may be incompetent. When action is necessary in a crisis, demonstrate the flaws in the model and communicate a plan of action—then just do it. Don't wait for a decision or permission from Rational PMs. You may not get one if they have reached analysis paralysis.

Idealist

Values
Authenticity and unique value of each individual, relationships

Typical leadership tendencies
Diplomatic, kind, and people-focused; may sacrifice end result for relationship

Under stress, leadership style may be perceived as
Emotional and overly democratic . Under stress, Idealist PMs may revert to "project management by majority vote." Issues and discontent may trigger emotional rather than logical reactions. Idealist PMs may appear "flaky"—making and then reversing decisions with seemingly no rationale. This may be exacerbated by polarization of the customer and project team (or even individual project team members) around an issue. Idealist PMs will find a reason to agree with who they are currently speaking with, appearing to change direction and decisions in real time. They may lose their big picture focus and obsess on minutiae.

Best approach to use when PM is under stress
Ask what you can do to support Idealist PMs. "What do you need from me?" Don't argue; help Idealist PMs regain their focus on the larger goal by providing a qualitative, personal "hook." Don't bother pointing out the inconsistencies in their decisions and/or actions—Idealist PMs will be able to articulately rationalize their actions, to their own satisfaction if not yours.

Temperament-Influenced Communication Styles

High-speed broadband internet transmission, cellular phones, and wireless PDAs have made today's communication instant, mobile, and globally accessible. But while the lines of transmission may be clear, frequently the messages we send are not.

The sacrifice of clarity and purpose in our messages is commonly the by-product of the digitized world we've created, depend upon, and come to love. Project managers must be engaged in the business of communication—not fiber optics or packet switching—but the simple art of talking/sending and understanding/receiving.

Enlightened project managers invoke the basic requirement for effective communication. They are continually challenged to build bridges between language and expression, cultural assumptions and misunderstandings, in order to ensure views are heard, understood, and considered.

Ultimately, project managers are responsible for transforming ideas into coordinated action and delivering a tangible result. The verbal sender—most vested in the message being received in the intended way—often forgets that the substance of the message depends entirely upon the receiver's interpretation. Transforming your message into productive action occurs only with an awareness about your own temperament and communication patterns with a view toward adapting your communication style to meet another's world-view.

Ideas are simply bundles of words.

- Project managers must understand how to design and produce an engaging word package.
- Project managers realize that "the package" determines the nature of the communication impression.
- Project managers must understand and practice the art of persuasion by being aware of their own temperament and style

and by adapting their style to meet the needs of the situation they need to have some impact on.

Exercise:

How do you tend to communicate?

You have just been advised by your lead designer that there is a crisis—your project team has encountered a show-stopping situation. No progress in the project can occur until the situation is resolved. You are the project manager. How will you communicate the status of the project to your boss? Answer the question for a boss of each of the four temperaments: Artisan, Guardian, Rational, and Idealist. (For helpful insights, refer to the temperament communication styles.)

The Myth of the
Perfect Project Manager

23

Does a "perfect" project manager exist?

Exercise:

Think of the projects you've worked on, and recall the project managers. Which ones did you like working with? Why? What did others on the team think of the PM?

Which ones were a challenge to work with? Why? What did others on the team think of the PM?

As we've seen, the needs of project team members can be extraordinarily diverse from the perspective of temperament. How can a single individual—the PM—foster an environment that meets the Temperament needs of team members?

To accomplish this task, a project manager would have to succeed in the following:

The "Perfect" Project Manager		
Embraces divergent thinking	yet	Drives convergent decision making
Stimulates debate	yet	Succeeds based on closure
Creates structure and order	yet	Makes room for "organized chaos"
Strives for team harmony	yet	Believes discord generates new ideas and deepens personal relationships over time
Thinks linearly	yet	Can take quantum leaps
Attempts to create a sense of team as "family"	yet	Respects the individuality and privacy of team members
Takes time to think, to discuss, and to plan	yet	Remains focused on action and results
Tolerates (even encourages) mistakes by team members	yet	Inspires ever higher levels of quality
Flexes his or her own style to accommodate the needs of others	yet	Remains true to temperament and takes care of his or her own needs
Understands and supports the needs of individual team members	yet	Understands and supports the needs of the team
Understands and can "play politics" effectively	yet	Is not politically motivated—is only motivated to lead the team to success
Creates a relaxed atmosphere to support optimum individual and team performance	yet	Drives the team hard against seemingly impossible deadlines

Exercise:

What other PM paradoxes can you identify?

The "Perfect" Project Manager
yet
yet
yet
yet
yet
yet
yet
yet
yet
yet
yet
yet
yet

Exercise:

For each paradox, circle the "half" that most closely fits your personal needs and temperament—what you would like your project manager and project team to focus on.

How can you as a project manager and your project team try to create an environment where you successfully "live the paradox" without creating undue project risk?

Identify one item that you would like to personally commit to and develop further.

Flight Crew Preparation

Helping Unique Individuals Form A Functioning Team

"All your strength is in union.
All your danger is in discord."
—Henry Wadsworth Longfellow

Putting It All Together

24

We've covered a lot of ground to reach this point. Now it's time to put it all together. How will your project team work together through the various stages of the project management process, best leveraging the valuable, diverse temperaments and talents on your team? We'll cover how to map your team's temperament composition, identify and discuss individual strengths and challenges throughout the project life cycle—including how to exploit team temperament synergies—and finally, how to launch and debrief a project, using a case study project team if you don't have a team of your own at the moment.

Mapping Your Project Team's Temperament Composition

Put the name of each member of your project team in the appropriate box. Where are there gaps? Is there a good balance of temperaments on your team? If not, what might you do to compensate? (Use the case study team if you are not currently on a project team.)

Idealist	**Guardian**
Rational	**Artisan**

Now let's look at the project management process and how you as an individual relate to it. With a better understanding of temperament, identify where you think you will have strengths and where you think you will have challenges. Identify the help you can offer, as well as the help you might like to request.

Project Management Process	Identify your strengths— what help can you offer others?	Describe your challenges—what help would you like from others?
Define a scope		
Develop a risk management plan		
Develop a communication plan		
Develop a quality management plan		
Request necessary resources		
Respond when the answer is no		
Hold or participate in meetings		
Handle a project crisis		
Assess changes		
Make recommendations regarding change		

Now let's see how an understanding of temperament can assist you in working with the team. You've met our team (see Appendix B), mapped the team's composition, and looked at your own strengths and challenges. Now let's see what some of the issues might be with this particular team as a whole.

Idealist	Guardian
Charles Kelly	Tammy Casey
Rational	Artisan
Kurt Ben	Julie Jane

What might be the strengths of this team?

What might be some possible challenges?

Revisit the phases of the project from the table in the last exercise. Identify who might show strengths in each phase and who might have challenges. How might you be able to help specific individuals?

Getting Ready
for Project Launch

25

At the start of each project it is important to have a formal start—a kickoff meeting to ensure everyone is clear and on the same page. The kickoff meeting presents the best opportunity to establish the project management methodology that will be used by the team, as well as to establish the team temperament profile and discuss the team's composition, strengths, and challenges. Although the bias is often to start the discussion with the concrete project and its needs, it is critical to start with temperament—the team members and their needs.

Investing the time to fully understand and employ the diverse working styles of team participants will help save time and energy for the duration of the project. Knowing—and addressing—individual team member's strengths and weaknesses will always help the team avoid the pitfalls that project teams often encounter. The individual and team exercises above can be used in a kickoff meeting to facilitate a team discussion, but there are many more questions that can be asked of the team to stimulate valuable dialogue.

Here are important questions that will give the team the means to ensure superior performance:

1. What is the best job you've ever had? Identify the qualities that made this job "the best."
2. What skills did you draw upon that made this job so rewarding?
3. While working in a team environment, what practices do you find most unnerving?
4. How do you like to receive direction? What type of information is important to you?
5. How would you like your manager to monitor your progress?
6. What are the greatest strength and greatest challenge you bring to a project team?
7. What are three characteristics you most value in a project manager?
8. How would you prefer to communicate (verbal/written) with the team?
9. Given the four options listed below, which one most closely describes your preferred decision-making process?
   - "I'll talk and I'll decide."
   - "We all talk and I decide."
   - "We all talk and we all decide."
   - "You talk and you decide."

Typically, when a project team meets for the first time, the discussion focuses on the task at hand: the project plan and the deliverables, assuming these have already been created. This discussion is often held at "ground zero"—looking at the lowest level of work to be done and making sure everyone understands his or her individual tasks. To best set the stage for a project launch, however, a top-down view of the project should be communicated by the project manager to the team. To ensure all stakeholders understand their role in and importance to the project, the customer, third-party suppliers, and the Project Team's management should participate in this project-centric part of the kickoff meeting, if at all possible.

Project topics to discuss should include all components of the project management methodology:

- Project goal
- Project objectives
- Project plan:
    - Activities
    - Tasks (If the project is large, leave tasks for smaller subteam meetings)
- Initial risk assessment (Brainstorm, preferably with a straw plan as the starting point)
- Identification of key stakeholders and their communication needs (Brainstorm, preferably with a straw plan as the starting point.)
- Quality planning
- Change control

As we've seen in observing temperament throughout the project life cycle, the conversation may become tangential, addressing the "what" and "who" of the process. Certain team members will be drawn to the visioning part of the meeting, while others will want to move quickly to discussions of purpose and timeline. Keeping the team dialogue on track is often difficult, and common direction and focus can be elusive. Holding the temperament portion of the kickoff meeting first allows the team to better self-facilitate through a self-awareness of styles and preferences, minimizing the effort required by either the PM or the meeting facilitator and maximizing the results of the meeting.

Project Debriefing

Just as important as a project kickoff meeting is a formal meeting to bring the project to a close. Once again, the meeting agenda should include a temperament component and a project component. During the debriefing, however, it is of value to reverse the order of these. By reviewing tangible project results first and allowing team members to pat themselves on the back for a job well done, they achieve a sense of closure. This allows the team to segue to the more personal and sometimes difficult task of self- and team-reflection.

Project agenda topics for the debriefing should closely parallel those of the kickoff meeting:

- Project goal: How well did we achieve what we set out to do?
- Project objectives: How well did we measure up—achieving results and making dates?
- Project plan: How well did we organize ourselves—both in planning and executing?
    - Activities
    - Tasks
- Risk management: How well did we anticipate and deal with risks?
- Communication management: How well did we identify stakeholders and interact with them?
- Quality: Was the customer satisfied with our results?
- Change control: How effectively did we manage change?
- Lessons Learned: What would we do differently next time?

For the temperament portion of the debriefing, the following questions can stimulate valuable discussion and help team members identify lessons to take to their next project.

1. What worked well about our team dynamics? What didn't work?
2. How well did we acknowledge individual working styles and leverage individual strengths?
3. How effectively did we mitigate conflict?
4. Was this a team experience that you would like to repeat?
5. If you were to repeat the process, what would you change?
6. What did you learn from this experience?
7. Might additional opportunities surface as a result of this project? Personally? For the organization? For the client?

Mission Accomplished!

*"We are each of us angels with only one wing,
and we can only fly by embracing one another."*
- Luciano de Crescenzo

Summary

We have now walked through the project management process and reviewed the behavior, reactions, and interactions of the temperaments along the way. You might wonder how any project ever finishes successfully! As we've seen, many projects don't. In one year alone, it is estimated American companies and government agencies will spend over $80 billion for canceled software projects—and that's just for software projects.

Burnout is high among project teams where stress levels reach excessive heights, yet a great deal of stress is self-inflicted by the absence of a robust project management process and by inadvertent temperament clashes among team members.

By following a simple yet rigorous project management process and by actively encouraging project teams to be aware of the affects of temperament on their reactions and interactions throughout the project life cycle, project teams have a higher likelihood of achieving that elusive goal: delivery of a value-added result to a satisfied customer by a happy project team.

Blank Project Management Frameworks

Scope Definition Framework

Project Name:	Project Manager:
Budget ($):	Budget Resources (Staff Hours):
Due Date: MM/DD/YYYY	

Project Goal:

. . . .

Major Features:

. . . .

Project Constraints:

. . . .

Quality Assessment:

. . . .

Risk Management Framework

No.	Risk	Likelihood	Risk Outcomes	Impact	Mitigators Avoid/Minimize	Reasses Date
1						
2						
3						
4						
5						
6						
7						
8						
9						
10						

Communication Management Framework

Task	Target Audience	Messages	Rationale	Communication Channel	Assigned To	Due Date, Trigger, or Frequency
1						
2						
3						
4						
5						
6						
7						
8						
9						
10						

Quality Management Framework

Quality Objectives:

Internal Inspections:

External / Customer Inspections:

Project Dashboard Framework

Project Name:
Project Manager:

Budget ($):
Resources (Staff Hours):

Due Date:
Dashboard Date:

Scope:

	# Change Reqs Submitted	Number Approved	Number Declined	Number Pending	% On Time Responses
This period					
Last period					
Project to date					

Budget: (Dollars, Resources, or both as needed)

	Actual to Date	Projected Future Spending	Projected Project Total	Scoped Project Budget	Variance
This period					
Last period					
Prior period					

Schedule:

	Target	Actual or Projected	Status
Major Milestones: 1. 2. 3. 4. 5.			
Major Deliverables: 1. 2. 3. 4. 5.			

Quality:

	Target	Actual or Projected	Status
Quality Objectives: 1. 2. 3. 4. 5.			
All Inspections: 1. 2. 3. 4. 5.			

Action Item Framework

Tracking Number	Date Opened	Action Item	Owner	Due Date	Status	Date Closed
1						
2						
3						
4						
5						
6						
7						
8						
9						
10						

Change Management Framework

Tracking Number:
Date Requested:
Requestor:

Circle all that apply:
Scope Change
Budget Change
Due Date Change
Quality Change

Request Description:

Reason for Request:

Project Analysis/Recommendation: **Date Submitted:**

Agreed Changes:

Scope:

Budget:

Due Date:

Quality:

_____   _____
Requester Signature / Date   **Project Manager Signature / Date**

Case Study

In this book, we will present and build on a case study to take a fictional project team through the project management process. As we do, they (and we) will learn about the application of temperament to the project team. Although the company and the characters are fictional, they are a typical mix of personalities and business challenges that anyone might encounter on a project.

The Company

Acme Corporation is a services provider whose value proposition is to offer PC (personal computer) support and repair for enterprises of all sizes. This model is both highly effective and quite lucrative—as the PC has become indispensable to workers in virtually every industry, every enterprise needs to ensure that its employees' PCs work round the clock.

The Acme support model has two major components:

- A centralized call center for incoming calls—called the Tier 1 support organization. The goal of the call center is to resolve all calls possible and, where resolution isn't possible, to collect the information necessary for Tier 2 support to respond.
- A distributed Field Support organization of PC hardware and software professionals—the Tier 2 support organization. When the call center hands off a trouble ticket to field support, the technician goes to the desk of the requester and resolves the problem.

Those enterprises that choose to provide their own PC support to their employees—whether by formally creating their own call center and field support organizations, or by encouraging PC-literate employees to help their fellow colleagues as best they can—typically pay more for inconsistent (if even measurable) results. Consequently, employees' PCs are unavailable to them for longer periods of time when there's a problem, and typically they are is given no time frame within which the problem might be resolved. These companies take a productivity hit and their employees are frustrated.

By consolidating call center support at a centralized, low-cost geographic location (Memphis), Acme is able to hire top-quality call center professionals at below-market salaries. A single call center professional can take calls from any incoming client, creating a highly efficient delivery model. Although field support, by the very nature of their job, are distributed geographically and located at or near client sites, Acme is able to keep costs down by partnering with regional vendors that have teams of highly trained and certified technicians. Through these strategic partnerships, Acme is able to commit to volume business with these vendors, and in return, the vendors offer Acme deep discounts on their services.

Acme offers its clients guaranteed levels of service (most importantly, time to resolution) and backs the guarantee by financial penalties paid by Acme if it is unable to perform to contractually defined levels of performance. Acme passes appropriate performance targets to its Field Support service partners and likewise establishes contractual penalty clauses with them, ensuring that everyone shares the same performance expectations and everyone is contractually (and financially) motivated to achieve them.

As a result of this value proposition, Acme's clients are able to outsource business functionality that is outside their core competency, improving worker productivity and reducing overhead.

The Project Context

Acme has just signed a five-year services contract with Bravo Insurance for ten of its major offices across the country—covering roughly

15,000 employees and a similar number of PCs. The deal represents $250M in revenue for Acme. The contract calls for a three-month transition of PC support services between Bravo and Acme—in three months, Acme must gradually take over all responsibility for all PC hardware and software support. At the end of the three-month interval, Acme must provide 24/7 support of all Bravo PCs in ten offices and meet the very aggressive levels of service outlined in the contract. If Acme misses any of these service level agreements beyond the three-month window, it must pay steep fines.

Acme plans to integrate Bravo's incoming call traffic into Acme's Memphis call center. Management reports indicate that the call center professionals have ample capacity to take the additional call volume and still meet their service level commitments. Several of Bravo's offices were out of the geographic areas served by Acme's existing field support partners, so for local field support, Acme entered into a new partnership with Capital PC Services. Conveniently, Capital and Acme were already in partnership discussions, and Capital covers all the cities outlined in the Bravo contract.

An Acme project team has been assembled to manage the transition project—the three-month transition of services from Bravo to Acme. This project includes the following key contractual obligations:

• Perform a physical inventory of all Bravo PC hardware and software.

Bravo did not keep accurate records of when PCs were acquired or updated or which offices have the equipment. Since the contract value was based on numbers and locations of PCs, the actual contract value and payments will be adjusted based on this information. Accurate PC inventory information is also required to dispatch the right technician to the right locations where Tier 2 support is required. Bravo plans spot audits of Acme's inventory to ensure 99.8 percent accuracy of inventory data.

• Transition support of one-third of the total PCs from Bravo to Acme during each month of the three-month transition period.

This is the most aggressive transition schedule Acme has signed to date. In prior contracts, Acme allowed two full months for planning prior to beginning the transition of support. The existing transition project plans are believed to already be fully optimized. The project team transitioning Bravo will be operating in uncharted territory. The presales technical support team strongly advised against this aggressive transition schedule—the team believes it is impossible to achieve.

• Meet all contractual service levels at the point a PC is transitioned to Acme, or pay contractual penalties.

In past deals, Acme successfully negotiated reduced service performance levels during the three-month transition period. This time Acme conceded—again counter to the arguments of the presales technical support team. Acme wanted to be the first PC services vendor to win a major customer in the insurance industry. If they hadn't conceded this point, Bravo had made it clear it would be a deal breaker.

A team of eight Acme colleagues, including the project manager, has been assigned to the Bravo transition project. Since Acme has been experiencing rapid growth due to the popularity of its service offering, several of the team members are new hires. They are not familiar with Acme's way of managing transition projects, and they don't know the other members of the project team. The new hires are unaware of the challenges they face due to the contractual arrangements with Bravo; the remaining transition team members are only too aware.

The Project Team

We will present eight personas that reflect the four temperaments and a few variations within each temperament. It is important to emphasize that we are all a little of each persona, however, temperament reflects a pattern of behavior that is always present.

Each team member is described from the point of view of Casey, the project manager. We will be revisiting these faces often throughout the project management process, so you can better understand how to work more effectively with your present constituency.

First Person: Guardian

Tammy: At her best, she is my superstar; at her worst, an intransigent witch.

Tammy gets things done efficiently and can be depended upon to complete the work exactly as it was originally conceived. She is experienced in project management, and creating structure and following a form comes naturally to her. She is thorough and precise. She has a solid understanding of our business objective, and she marshals resources and manages time and the process to deliver the end result.

For example, over the weekend I woke up in the middle of the night realizing that the requested client change would impact a major area of the project and could lead to extraordinary cost overruns. I panicked and tried to think of a quick fix. When I got back to the office on Monday, Tammy had already done preliminary work on the same topic and come up with a workable contingency plan. I sleep better at night knowing she is on the team.

She works well with the team but won't tolerate someone who is not pulling his or her weight. She gets frustrated from time to time when someone tries to circumvent the process. She tends to assume more than her share of the workload, but when overworked, she complains and faults others for not delivering results.

She expects the team members to respect one another as well as the client. She expects everyone on the team to fully understand his or her role and responsibilities. Her brilliant planning ability saves time in the long run, but some team members become frustrated with the amount of time she invests in preparation and the attention to detail that she demands. While she can solve tough problems, her solutions are neither earth-shattering nor particularly original. She relies on thoughtful, tried-and-true methods.

Again, Tammy is my superstar.

Second Person: Idealist

Julie: She is enthusiastic at her best; scatterbrained at her worst.

Julie is new to the organization. I embrace her enthusiasm and wish I could bottle it and serve it to other people in the organization. She is creative, usually generating innovative ideas. Somewhat unconventional in her method, her passion and energy are inspiring. She helps others transcend the accepted norm.

She has an unusual ability to motivate people, inspiring them to participate in the most mundane tasks. She has the ability to sell any idea or product. I have watched her function as an engaging and effective interface between individuals, displaying her ability to build bridges between disparate viewpoints.

Julie's challenge is learning to negotiate from strength, learning to cooperate without capitulation—establishing a realistic middle ground and developing reasonable and mutually rewarding goals for all concerned.

She is tireless during the promotion and initiation of new ideas. Often drawn to unconventional ways of doing things, she can easily derail a project and confound her colleagues. She usually overloads herself in an attempt to execute every "great idea," and she needs help prioritizing her "to-do" list. A nonlinear thinker, follow-through and closure are two of her fundamental challenges.

Third Person: Rational

Kurt: At his best, he is Mr. Brilliant; at his worst, Mr. Nitpicker.

Kurt possesses a complex intelligence that causes him to challenge the status quo. His questions inspire the group to find unusual and occasionally unique solutions. He works toward perfecting the process, improving the systems, illuminating what is unknown. Never satisfied, he holds himself and the team to the highest of standards.

With his goal in mind, he charts a precise course. Kurt is a conceptual thinker with an extraordinary breadth and depth of knowledge. He operates based on deep and penetrating insights regarding his vision of the future.

His expertise is essential to the team's success; he is able to integrate multidisciplinary perspectives. His ability to analyze data and execute to strategy is well known throughout the organization.

He is a tough guy to work with, often overlooking the skill and talent of others. Once he regards you as incompetent, he quickly dismisses your input. Some people on the team perceive him as arrogant. His critical thinking skills are both an asset and a liability. When stressed, he becomes more controlling, often instigating a systematic dissection of all aspects of the project.

Fourth Person: Artisan

Charles: Superhero or saboteur.

Cool in a crisis, Charles knows exactly what to do "in the moment" to solve a problem. His technical savvy and ability to design a quick fix make him well-known and admired by his peers and customers. Basing his decisions on concrete, logical data, Charles mistrusts the subjective, emotional decisions of others.

Like a superhero, he invents "workarounds" to the most thorny problem, often maneuvering around the process, structure, and rules. I can always depend upon on him to deliver a result, despite the fact that it might not be the one we had originally envisioned.

Charles thrives in a fast-paced environment and can change his perspective in the blink of an eye. He thrives on chaos and becomes bored easily by redundancy, rarely approaching tasks the same way twice. Despite the risk of a negative reaction, Charles is capable of sabotaging existing project processes in the absence of tangible progress.

He enjoys challenge. The words "it can't be done" inspire and ignite Charles to develop inventive ways to resolve the problem. He has a reputation for "saving the day" when things go awry.

Charles becomes impatient with too much structure. Charles is known to say "It depends" whenever you ask him how he will do something. Sometimes others perceive him as contemptuous of protocol, clearly more comfortable and effective operating within his own set of rules and trusting his own instincts.

Fifth Person: Artisan

Kelly: Mr. Party or Mr. Party Pooper.

Kelly brings positive energy and a sense of fun to the team. Known as one of the best and the brightest, he brings inventive and satisfying solutions to customer and organizational issues. He has superior people skills and is equally adept with project-oriented tasks. Both prompt and practical, he and Charles share an appreciation for a fast-paced environment.

Action oriented and priding himself on delivering results, Kelly doesn't need the details, he just wants the gist of information. The balance he can figure out himself.

Kelly needs to know why we are working on something and how it will be used. Otherwise, he doesn't want to invest his effort. He is sensitive to people's feelings and tends to avoid conflict. Trying to please everyone, he frequently overextends himself and underestimates constraints in place.

Whether he is appointed as the team leader or assumes an unauthorized leadership role, the team seems comfortable following Kelly's lead. His "get things going" style can be inspiring, and the group seems to see him as the center of action.

I'm concerned that in the face of disillusionment or despair, he might cease participating in the project ("take his marbles and go home"). His last manager mishandled this situation by micromanaging Kelly, who, in turn, led the team in some undesirable directions, causing the project to ultimately fail.

I know Kelly is a smart and valuable member of the team, if only I can channel his energy toward a positive result.

Sixth Person: Idealist

Jane: Miss Mentor or Pathetic Princess.

Jane creates a nurturing and energetic team environment, bringing out the best in people. A skilled communicator, Jane is able to use diverse and effective strategies. She is able to teach others and shows great patience with individuals who don't share her competencies.

Jane is talented at resolving team politics that can impede transition and, ultimately, a project's success.

She employs a directive manner of speaking but maintains a softness that gently guides people in the direction she wants. I've known Jane for many years and have learned to appreciate her ability to deal with individuals effectively.

I have also experienced Jane at her worst. For example, she has a need for others' approval, which can displace her better judgment. Once, when requested to extend a "hard" deadline on a very visible project, Jane approved the extension because of a tearful plea, despite knowing the missed deadline would have severe ramifications. Later when I asked her why she did that, she said she really identified with the requester's problem and really wanted that person to like her.

As you can see, Jane has a problem establishing and maintaining boundaries.

Seventh Person: Rational

Ben: The Inventor or Mr. Apathy.

With a preference for idea generation over implementation, Ben shares a talent for thinking strategically with Kurt. Each can spend hours pondering complex problems, and they thoroughly enjoy debating one another over whose idea is superior.

Ben's focus is "possibility," and he often envisions a future with a foundation beyond traditional norms. (A key player in the organization, Ben was the one who initially created this new opportunity and raised money for the project.)

Unrestrained in his creativity, polished and precise in his word choice, Ben is a charismatic character.

At times, he can overthink a problem, easily slipping into "analysis-paralysis." For example, after developing the current contracts for the client, he realized that his model would function brilliantly only in an ideal scenario. Ben failed to set realistic expectations around actually following the plan in an imperfect environment. He is self-critical in the face of his lack of foresight, and he is becoming even less able to function as he contemplates his mistake.

He is his own worst critic and his own best advocate. Logical and objective in his analysis, he can transform the ordinary into the extraordinary. When he's paired with someone possessing a talent for execution, his visions can and will be actualized.

Eighth Person: Guardian

Casey, the project manager: Miss Team Builder, Miss Triangulation.

I value a harmonious team environment and act as the caretaker of the group..

I appreciate diversity and think I'm a good judge of people's strengths and weaknesses. Making sure my team is happy and working well together is what I value most. I base my success on that, but I also need to make sure that the tasks are accomplished.

I have been leading project teams for many years, and although I don't have the same systematic or organizational skills as my superstar, I appreciate and have discovered that I do better when I have a structure and process to follow. I need to be part of a team. I was once an individual contributor and found I hated working in a vacuum.

I enjoy having parties to celebrate our success and give my team plaques and recognition awards. This embarrasses some members of the team. But I think it is important. I expect respect for my position and have earned my title from the school of hard knocks. I get frustrated and won't tolerate disrespect to anyone. I protect my team at all costs. I stand up for my team in the organization, and generally I think people like working for me.

If anyone has a complaint about me, it would probably be that I tend to manage by consensus and am too soft-hearted.

I don't like to admit it, but when I feel stressed or undermined, I can gossip and "stir the pot" so that people distrust each other and then come to me, since I'm the authority. Actually, a little discontent among the ranks assists me in maintaining my authority.

This is a complex project, but leading this team should be interesting because I have diverse personalities, talents, levels of experience, knowledge, and skill sets working for me.

I find it enormously satisfying when we deliver concrete, tangible results and get rewarded for it.

Wish me luck.

Bibliography

Berens, Linda V. *Understanding Yourself and Others®: An Introduction to Temperament*. Huntington Beach: Telos Publications, 1998.

Campbell, Scott. *Quick Guide to the Four Temperaments for Peak Performance*. Huntington Beach: Telos Publications, 2003.

Cooper, Brad. *Quick Guide to the Four Temperaments and Sales*. Huntington Beach: Telos Publications, 2003.

Daniel, Wayne W; Terrel, James C. *Business Statistics*. Houghton Mifflin.

Delunas, Eve. *Survival Games Personalities Play*. Sunflower, Inc. 1992.

Dunning, Donna. *Quick Guide to the Four Temperaments and Learning*. Huntington Beach: Telos Publications, 2003.

Isachsen, Olaf, and Linda Berens, *Working Together*. Coronado: Neworld Management Press, 1988.

Kasmier, Leonard J. *Schaum's Outline of Theory and Problems of Business Statistics*. New York: McGraw-Hill Professional.

Keirsey, David and Marilyn Bates. *Please Understand Me*. Del Mar: Prometheus Nemesis Books, 1978.

Keirsey, David. *Portraits of Temperament*. Del Mar: Prometheus Nemesis Books, 1987.

Keirsey, David. *Please Understand Me II*. Del Mar: Prometheus Nemesis Books, 1998.

Kerr, Steven. Ultimate Rewards: *What Really Motivates People to Achieve*. Harvard Business Review Book Series, Boston, MA: Harvard Business School Press, 1997.

Knutson, Joan. *Project Management for Business Professionals: A Comprehensive Guide*. New York: John Wiley & Sons, Inc., 2001.

Knutson, Joan; Bitz, Ira. *Project Management: How to Plan and Manage Successful Projects*. New York: NY AMACOM Books, 1991.

Lewis, James P. *Fundamentals of Project Management*. New York: AMACOM Books, 1995.

McLeary, Joseph Webb. *By the Numbers: Using Facts and Figures to Get Your Projects and Plans Approved*. New York: AMACOM.

Myers, Isabel Briggs and Peter B. Myers. *Gifts Differing*. Palo Alto: Consulting Psychologists Press, Inc., 1980.

Nardi, Dario. *Multiple Intelligences and Personality Type*. Huntington Beach: Telos Publications, 2001.

Ryan, Thomas P. *Statistical Methods for Quality Improvement*. New York: John Wiley & Sons, Inc., 2000.

Taylor, James, *A Survival Guide for Project Managers*. New York: AMACOM Books, 1998.

A Guide to the Project Management Body of Knowledge (PMBOK® guide), North Carolina, PMI Publishing, 2000.

Pinto, Jeffrey K. *The Project Management Institute: Project Management Handbook*. Jossey-Bass Business & Management Series, 1998.

Project Management Institute. *Practice Standard for Work Breakdown Structures*. Project Management Institute, 2001.

Tieger, Paul D. and Barbara Barron-Tieger. *Do What You Are*. Canada: Little Brown & Co., 1992.